Human Rights

Voices of World's Young Activists

Human Rights
Voices of World's Young Activists

Amii Omara-Otunnu, Sergio Mobilia and
Bandana Purkayastha

frontpage

frontpage
www.frontpagepublications.com

First published 2012

Frontpage Publications Limited
13 John Prince's Street, 2nd Floor, London W1G 0JR, United Kingdom

Frontpage
Level 6, Constantia
11 Dr U N Brahmachari Sarani, Kolkata 700017, India

British Library Cataloguing in Publication Data
A catalogue record for this book is available from the British Library

ISBN: 978 93 810430 6 6

Printed in India
by Sadhana Press Private Limited
76 B B Ganguli Street, Kolkata 700012

Typeset by Compuset International
85 Park Street, Kolkata 700016

Contents

Bio-sketch of the Contributors vi

Foreword xiii

Human Rights, Global Visions 1
Bandana Purkayastha

Sixty Years of Relentless Human Rights Activism 9
Sergio Mobilia

HUMAN TRAFFICKING & SECURITY 15

Human Rights and the Problem of Trafficking 17
Arpine Kostanyan

The Commercial Sexual Exploitation of Children and Human Trafficking 26
Lindsay McNicholas

Post-Conflict Multicultural Societies and the Concept of Human Security 32
Elena Mihajlova

CHILDREN & YOUTH IN POVERTY OR CONFLICT ZONES 39

Youth Participation and Post-Conflict Recovery in Northern Uganda 41
Awici Charles Churchill

State of Peace, Promises for Nepal's Children 53
Amiya Bhatia

Together for the Betterment of Street Children 62
Phearun Kuch

ENVIRONMENTALISM & EARTH-CARE 69

Political Participation, Youth and the Environment 71
Lina Mata Guido

Human Rights and the Environment 80
Vannaphone Manibod

FOOD SECURITY & HEALTH 83

A Kenyan Perspective on Hunger, Malnutrition and Human Rights 85
Dickens Osano Molo

The Right to Food in the Light of the Millennium Development Goals and the Universal Declaration of Human Rights 94
Angelina Reif

The Internet as a Means of Bringing Information on HIV/AIDS to the African Population 104
Andrea Labruto

ON THE LEGAL PROTECTION OF NON-HETERONORMATIVE IDENTITIES 113

The Right of Homosexual People to Marry and Establish their Own Families 115
Haksym Chhay

THE USE OF LEGAL INSTRUMENTS FOR SOCIAL JUSTICE 121

The Law as a Tool for Social Change 123
Raquel Nunes

Locating the Individual in the Universal Declaration of Human Rights 132
Aheli Purkayastha

Are the UN Millennium Development Goals the Solution to World Problems? 137
Beatriz Borges Urrutia

HUMAN RIGHTS EDUCATION 141

Hope for a Brighter Future 143
Nerina Maqueira

Peace Education as a Tool for the Reinforcement of Human Rights and Fundamental Freedoms 154
Nermine Mounir

Building a Community of Learners 162
Arcie G Mallari

In Pursuit of a Global Education 166
Sara Minkara

Notes 169

Index 177

Bio-sketch of the Contributors

Aheli Purkayastha currently works at the Global Policy Forum in New York, **USA**. Since her college days at *Bryn Mawr College*, USA and University of Edinburgh, Scotland, Aheli has been working on a variety of social justice matters primarily related to race issues.

Amiya Bhatia, studying Social Anthropology at the *University of Cambridge*, **UK**, has worked for the NGOs in India, Nepal and the United Kingdom. Amiya's focused areas are children's right, peace education, post-conflict issues and youth participation.

Andrea Labruto, from **Italy**, is a former President of the *Italian Medical Students Association* (*SISM*), Editor of the *Publishing Group*, and an active member of the *International Federation of Medical Students' Associations* (*IFMSA*).

Angelina Reif, from **Austria**, volunteers with the NGO *Save Tibet* as political and public affairs advisor. Angelina is passionate about promoting human rights and drawing attention to deplorable political and social circumstances through dialogue.

Arcie Mallari is the Founder and President of *Silid Aralan, Inc* (*SAI*), working in the field of children and youth development in Payatas, Quezon City, **Philippines**.

Arpine Kostanyan is involved in youth works and represents *Federation of Youth Clubs of* ***Armenia***. Arpine's focused areas include: human rights, sustainable development, gender issues, intercultural relations, European citizenship, immigration and integration.

Awici Charles Churchill, formerly associated with *Norwegian Refugee Council* in Uganda, is currently the Information and Protection Trainee in **Colombia**, South America. A Visiting Lecturer in Peace and Conflict Studies at the *Institute of Peace and Strategic Studies,* Gulu University, Uganda, Awici's thrust areas are the challenges faced by IDPs and refugees globally.

Beatriz Borges Urrutia is a Partner and Academic Director of the *Instituto de Mejoramiento y Capacitación del Abogado (IMCA)* in **Venezuela**. Beatriz has developed innovative course designs and interactive teaching in international human rights and public interest law. Beatriz is now working as an International Consultant in the United States and has litigated cases in domestic courts and the Inter-American System.

Dickens Osano Molo is attached at *World Vision International* working in the field of Human Nutrition, Health and Community Development in Kisumu, besides being a board member and advisor for several community based organisations in **Kenya**.

Elena Mihajlova, involved in teaching International Law and International Relations, is now President of the *Institute of Human Rights Partenij Zografski – Skopje*, Republic of **Macedonia**.

Haksym Chhay was one of the participants representing **Cambodia** at the *4th Global Intergenerational Leadership Training Programme*, held on 2-11 August 2008 at the University of Connecticut, USA.

Lina Mata Guido, hailing from **Costa Rica**, works as Executive Coordinator of the Leadership Programme 'Agents of Change' supported by the *Friedrich Ebert Foundation* (*FES*), Germany. Lina's work focuses on democracy, youth participation, gender mainstreaming and environmental protection in Central America.

Lindsay McNicholas works as a Resource Advocate for Denver Public Schools, Colorado, **USA** dealing with basic resources for children and families in poor and immigrant urban communities. Lindsay investigated the growing sex-trafficking industry vis-a-vis human rights situations in Cambodia.

Nerina Maqueira with her educational background in *Educational Psychology* has been working with teenagers *from disadvantaged backgrounds in* Buenos Aires, **Argentina**.

Nermine Mounir worked as a Registration Assistant, *UNHCR* to help the asylum-seekers in the Middle Eastern conflicts. Involved in peace education programme, Nermine is currently attached to *Alwan and Awtar*, a local NGO, to strengthen the intellectual, spiritual, moral, social and emotional development of children in the MENA region in **Egypt**.

Phearun Kuch works for *Friends-International*, an organisation attending to the needs of vulnerable children and youth, their families and societies in **Cambodia**.

Raquel Nunes is a team coordinator at the *Poles of Citizenship Programme* (*Programa Pólos de Cidadania*) in Belo Horizonte, **Brazil**.

Sara Minkara, from **Lebanon**, diagnosed with macular degeneration at the young age of 7, is an active member of the *National Federation for the Blind* (*NFB*), USA. In addition to promoting blind awareness, Sara also serves for *Al-Muslimat*, a Muslim organisation at *Wellesley College*, Wellesley, USA.

Sergio Mobilia, formerly an Associate to the UNESCO Chair & Institute of Comparative Human Rights, University of Connecticut, USA, now works as a senior analyst with Google, **Argentina**.

Vannaphone Manibod works for *Handicap International Belgium* in **Laos**. Vannaphone has been interested in peace building and passionate about making life better for the poor and marginalised in society.

Foreword

Today, we live in an epoch when technological revolution has woven together hitherto disparate parts of the world into mutual interdependence: a world in which the notion of a global village is no longer simply a metaphor of expression but a substantial reality of life. It is a global village where an outbreak of the SARS (Severe Acute Respiratory Syndrome) in Asia can spread panic in other regions of the world within days; where the onset of mad cow disease in Europe can trigger fear in the Americas and Japan instantaneously; where the Structural Adjustment policies of the World Bank and International Monetary Fund can wreak havoc in villages in Africa and Asia; where concerts to raise awareness about global warming can be conducted simultaneously in every region of the world; and where one can eat Chinese, Ethiopian, French, Indian, Italian or Japanese cuisine in any part of the world.

The challenge to foster a sustainable culture of human rights in the interdependent global village we live in is essentially threefold. It is, first, about how to devise means to share information about best practices and strategies globally. Second, it is about how to fashion methods of reciprocal learning and sharing of experiences, skills and knowledge, not only among leaders of the same generation, but also between those of different generations. And third, the challenge is also about to form a network of solidarity to support and reinforce the different human rights activities carried out in various regions of the world.

In the past several years, the UNESCO Chair & Institute of Comparative Human Rights has risen to the challenge by conducting a ten-day Global Intergenerational Leadership Programme annually at the University of Connecticut, USA. Organised as a forum, each year we bring together approximately seventy-five young leaders from various regions of the world to Connecticut, where, in a pastoral atmosphere, they engage in dialogue on various issues with more seasoned human rights practitioners and leaders.

The immediate principal objectives of conducting intergenerational dialogues, sharing and learning are to hone and sharpen leadership skills that would enhance effective engagement to foster a global culture of human rights. However, because the forum is inspired by the notion of human rights as *practical idealism* and grounded in *informed empathy*, participants are challenged to transcend their provincial conditioning and encouraged to blend idealism with the practical applications for three main human rights reasons. The first is to nudge participants to realise that rhetoric or words – or even concern – are no substitute for corrective actions and deeds of compassion that touch the lives of people, one at a time. The second is to cultivate and heighten faith and hope for fairer and more fraternal conditions in which human dignity and respect are accorded to all, regardless of social backgrounds. The third is to get participants to embrace values that align with the sentiments expressed by the poet, W B Yeats: "we are bred to a better thing than triumph." Put less poetically, we challenge participants to realise that for the sake of a common humanity, it might be judicious to de-emphasise the fetishes of materialism and raw politics in the world.

Of course, the work of the UNESCO Chair & Institute of Comparative Human Rights is carried within and in line with the framework and mandate of UNESCO's Constitution, which is committed to building peace in the minds and hearts of people. The Constitution itself spells out unambiguously the main tasks, thus:

> That the wide diffusion of culture, and the education of humanity for justice and liberty and peace are indispensable

> to the dignity of man and constitute a sacred duty which all the nations must fulfil in a spirit of mutual assistance and concern.
>
> That a peace based exclusively upon the political and economic arrangements of governments would not be a peace which could secure the unanimous, lasting and sincere support of the peoples of the world, and that the peace must, therefore, be founded, if it is not to fail, upon the intellectual and moral solidarity of mankind.

It is in this context that the essays in this publication should be read and understood. In fact, the essays are an outgrowth of the UNESCO Chair Global Intergenerational Forum of 2008. The idea behind publishing the essays of these young human rights leaders is based on a two-fold presumption. The first is that young leaders might have more imaginative insights into the new world that is emerging than their predecessors. The second is that, if we are to focus meaningfully on issues that will determine the welfare of humanity, we should listen to young leaders who will shape the course of history.

On procedural matter, it should be noted that after the essays were initially selected, participants were then asked to revise them for a wider readership beyond the conference attendees, under sub-headings that would make them easier for the reader to follow. The following were the suggested guidelines given to the writers to help them clarify their ideas and organise their essays:

- PROBLEM IDENTIFICATION: To define the issue or problem that the essay is attempting to answer; then to spell out the nature of the problem and why it is important for the reader to learn about it.

- HUMAN RIGHTS FRAMEWORK: To outline the larger intellectual and regional (or global) framework of human rights debates in which the problem is being considered and to indicate why the problem identified should indeed fall under the umbrella of human rights. In addition, each writer was asked to bring the essay to life by illustrating how the problem affects the self-fulfilment and dignity of particular individuals and groups, and to discuss broadly the relevance of the problem to human rights by citing relevant human rights instruments (documents).

- CROSS-REFERENCE OR COMPARATIVE ANALYSIS: Wherever possible, the writers were requested to find out whether the problem under discussion has been written about in a different region of the world; and if so, what were the manifestations of the problems in different cultural or material contexts? How, if at all, did people in a different region of the world deal with a similar problem? What do approaches by other people tell us about best practices in tackling the identified challenges?

- LOOKING FORWARD AS A YOUTH: Each young human rights leader was encouraged to look to the future and to try to telescope how bad or good the problem will be? The following questions were posed to the young leaders: Do you have hope that the problem will be tackled effectively? And, what role should young people play in fashioning solutions to the problem you have identified? Are there examples of young people engaging proactively to tackle similar problems, which can be used as model or inspiration? Here, each writer was encouraged to present a wide and international range of young voices on how to achieve particular human rights and to suggest some novel ideas by and for the next generation of human rights activists and thinkers.

- PROPOSAL FOR POSSIBLE SOLUTION: Having discussed the problem, each writer was asked to think about affirmative or positive ways to solve or at least ameliorate the problem. In particular, in the context of UNESCO's mandate, each writer was encouraged to give examples where people were being organised and their consciousness was being raised through education.

- CONCLUSION: Finally, each writer was asked, in the context of the 60th anniversary of the Universal Declaration of Human Rights (UDHR), to try to answer the question (as per the 1993 Vienna Programme of Action) whether human rights are interdependent, inter-related, indivisible and universal or relativistic.

The process of revising the essays was supervised by Sergio Mobilia, an Associate of the UNESCO Chair, who also served as over-all editor. Throughout, Sergio approached the task of editing the essays with an admirable degree of high professionalism and diligence. We, therefore, owe a sincere debt of gratitude to Sergio for his commitment and dedication and for finding the formula to get all the writers to revise in a more or less uniform and timely manner. But the essays would not have seen the light of day had it not been for the persistence and resourcefulness of Professor Bandana Purkayastha, who sought and negotiated with Abhijit Mazumder of Frontpage Publications Limited, London to make him willing to place faith in the ideas explored by these young human rights leaders from various regions of the world, as well as made requisite arrangements for publication. By her practical engagement to expand the frontiers of human rights, Professor Purkayastha has indeed demonstrated her extraordinary capacity to be a role model for the cause of global human rights.

In the UNESCO Chair's Office, we would like to thank Nana Amos, UNESCO Chair Programme Manager, who has been the linchpin of our activities. Over the years, Nana has done much to demonstrate her commitment to the wide-ranging agenda for human rights we have pursued, by being involved in virtually everything we have achieved. And, of course, last but not least, we are most grateful to the young human rights leaders who devoted time and resources to bring refreshing perspectives on the various issues that affect the future of human rights. There is no doubt that these essays make enormous contribution to the debates about the various human rights and, accordingly, enrich our understanding of these issues. It has been a privilege to share the experiences and analyses of these young leaders on whose shoulders the future of human rights rests. By their sense of purpose and commitment to focus on the issues they have tackled with the intention of translating the ideals of human rights into the lives of people, the young leaders have demonstrated with the enthusiasm of youth that they are ready to seize the moment for a stream of unlimited possibilities that lie ahead of them as they go forth. If these are the young people upon whom we pin our hopes for a better world, we can rest assured by their inspiration that we shall not give up our affirmative dreams, which are the essence of our common humanity. Indeed, these essays do much to renew our faith and keep the flame of human rights alight globally.

24 October 2011 Amii Omara-Otunnu

Human Rights, Global Visions

Bandana Purkayastha

I can think of no other way of introducing these essays than by placing them within a historical framework of human rights' visions and struggles. The voices of these activists are part of a stream of human rights Enterprise, a term I borrow from my friends Davita Glasberg and William Armaline (Armaline, Glasberg and Purkayastha 2011). As part of an enterprise, human rights are not simply about laws, they are also about the imaginations and actions of people and groups who claim rights and challenge the boundaries that keep diverse human beings from accessing these rights. But first, the history.

* * *

On 10 December 1948, when the United Nations released the Universal Declaration of Human Rights (UDHR), the document reflected the imprint of many people around the world.[1] At that time, the world was haunted by the images of the concentration camps and the atrocities committed against Jews in the name of nationalism. People who put in a great deal of effort into creating these human rights were driven to redress other injustices as well. Representatives from former and existing colonies talked about the impunity with which colonial powers subjugated people and societies around the world, politically, economically, socially, in order to create and maintain their own economic prosperity and political pre-eminence. The colonised were tired of killings, lack of political liberty, of economic repression, and depletion of their resources to fulfil the needs of the colonial powers, including support for *their* war efforts. People were tired of wars, of the unprecedented numbers of people who had been killed in World War II, as well as the economic deprivations, including deadly famines that resulted from procurement of food for the troops. A vast number of people were tired of racism; they spoke out against ideologies and institutions that classified individual human beings as less than a person, of policies that froze human beings into segregated, severely restricted social locations bereft of life chances that the racially privileged, of internments, of life imprisonments for demanding freedom.

The road to UDHR was rocky. Since inception this declaration is tied to the political struggles over the creation of the United Nations and its charter. In 1941, prior to the formation of the United Nations, the United States of America and United Kingdom had jointly produced the Atlantic Charter that proclaimed, among other matters, the right of all people to choose their governments, and their right to live free of want and fear. Yet, as World War II intensified and spread to new arenas of the globe, there was little evidence that such proclaimed principles were actually being used as a framework for action. In 1944, representatives of the USA, UK, Union of Soviet Socialist Republics, and China met at Dumbarton Oaks, and, despite many other conflicts over visions and policies – especially with the Chinese over matters of racial inequality – they agreed that these four powers should take up the major responsibility for maintaining peace and security across the world. They drew up a blueprint for the United Nations with a powerful Security Council, a council where these 'Big Four' would have permanent membership and veto power, along with a General Assembly, and an International Court of Justice. In this formulation, states' sovereignty would be sacrosanct. This articulation distinctly excluded the proposed United Nations organisation from having the powers to enforce human rights.

Not surprisingly, other countries were extremely critical of the Dumbarton Oaks agreement. Peter Frazer and Walter Nash (of New Zealand) proved to be tireless opponents of the arrangement that would have given all powers to politically powerful countries and trusted them to look after the interests of all others. Latin American countries, especially, Uruguay, Mexico, Brazil, Venezuela, Guatemala, Panama, complained against the proposed arrangements pointing to their long history of exploitation by the Northern powers. Leaders in colonised countries such as India raised questions about political freedom and racial equality. Women's rights leaders – such as Minerva Bernadino of the Dominican Republic – spoke on behalf of women's rights. A large number of individuals and non-governmental organisations (NGOs) – secular and religious NGOs – joined in the criticisms as well. Peace, justice, rule of law, democracy, non discrimination, right to self-determination of all people including indigenous groups and racial minorities, protection of the vulnerable during the war, emerged as crucial demands. The fulcrum of these demands was the idea of a United Nations Organisation where all countries would be equal and these countries would be collectively responsible for the fulfilment of the articulated demands for peace, justice, equality, and institutions to ensure lives of human dignity. As more diverse groups began to demand such an organisation, the governments who had drawn up the provisions at Dumbarton Oaks, came up with their own proposals. In the end, the United Nations charter, with its organisational features of an Assembly and a Security Council composed of Permanent Members with veto power, along with elected members, reflect that realist compromise between ideals, hopes and political realities. The declaration that begins with "We the people" includes the statement that nothing in the charter authorises the United Nations to intervene in matters of domestic jurisdiction.

The crafting of the UDHR was buffeted by the same conflicts over individual freedoms versus national interests. As more and more countries began to demand independence from colonial powers, NGOs, individuals, and representatives from countries – such as India, China, Philippines, Poland, Panama – spoke out against apartheid, racism and colonialism in the United Nations General Assembly. The Nuremburg trials brought fresh urgency to the need for protection of individuals against government atrocities. The earlier discussions of the objectives and principles that led to the United Nations Charter had already indicated a felt need for an array of political, civil, economic, social and cultural rights. But the demands for these rights became a cause of concern to some countries, expressly on the grounds of national sovereignty. Countries that were willing to speak about rights in principle, or protest against rights violations in other countries, were extremely reluctant to have their own records subject to similar scrutiny. The politics of the Cold War further shaped the context in which the UDHR was crafted. At the same time, hopeful of new changes to international political template, individuals and groups had begun to write to members of the commission that were crafting the UDHR, describing, often in harrowing terms, the violations they experienced. But the eighteen member commission – consisting of the representatives of Byelorussia, France, Panama, Philippines, the USSR, the United States (who worked on the declaration), Chile, China, Egypt, Lebanon, the United Kingdom, Yugoslavia (who worked on the convention), and Australia, India, Iran, Ukraine and Uruguay (who worked on methods of implementation) – and the chair, Eleanor Roosevelt, brought the UDHR to fruition in December 1948. The visionary text raised economic, cultural, and social rights to the level of the more recognisable political and civil rights; it made the case of a large number of hitherto vulnerable groups – like indigenous people – visible. Even as it allowed states to use the national sovereignty arguments, this declaration formalised a vision that we continue to struggle to realise today.

* * *

It is important to restate this history – of the international participation, of struggles, victories and setbacks – because many dominant voices in human rights scholarship have tended to simplify the history of these rights over the years. This simplification is partly due to repeated emphases on certain events, histories and people. It is also due to a hierarchical structure of knowledge dissemination – whose voices and accounts are most likely to be heard and quoted repeatedly – so that the contributions, visions, struggles and sacrifices of others rarely surface in accounts of human rights. Thus it is entirely possible to read scholarly accounts of human rights as part of a linear evolution from the Enlightenment, establishment of Western democracies to human rights (Donnelly 2003; for opposing scholarly views see, for instance, Sardar *et al* 1993, Pearce 2001). Scholars who trace human rights to unique roots in Western thought and practice typically focus wholly on a legalistic notion of rights without engaging with the visions, struggles and institutions that address and create social structural arrangements for the construction of lives of human dignity in other parts of the world (Sen 1998). The narrowly defined lineage of human rights has also been fostered by other entities as well. Some non-Western governments have argued that human rights are a 'Western' invention, and consequently not applicable to their societies. At local levels, groups have used the argument about upholding cultural human rights to 'normalise' their abuse of women, children, and other vulnerable groups in their midst. These governments and groups have actively drawn exclusionary boundaries to exclude whoever they do not consider to be 'equally human'.

Human rights are, however, not simply a matter of legal rights, though these are a significant brick in the edifice of human rights. As scholars such as Evelyn Nakano Glenn (2002) have discussed, rights are envisioned through persistent ideologies about who is worthy of such rights (and who are not), and the actions of powerful people to enforce inclusions and exclusions in everyday life. For instance, segregated residential areas are often maintained long after laws are dismantled due to the flight of white families as non-white families move into an area. In societies where women are encouraged to 'stay safe' within their homes, everyday sexual harassment and violence in public places ensure they are most likely to 'freely choose' to stay at home. Equally important, rights are established through organised claims for such rights. Despite its important role in formalising the idea that individuals have the right to live lives of dignity irrespective of the governments who hold political power over them, UDHR did not appropriately address the rights of women. It required several decades of organising by women's groups to establish women's rights as human rights. The convention on elimination of discrimination against women (CEDAW) was passed in 1993, and even now, the process of ensuring women's human rights is not complete (Cook 1994, Erturk 2005, Purkayastha 2008).

Thus, this book captures a stage in this history of struggle for human rights. It represents the visions and understanding of human rights – the violations of human dignity and the possible solutions and futures of a generation far removed from the mid-twentieth century.

Collectively, these essays tell us about contemporary understandings of who is considered to be human, who should have access to rights, which are these rights, and which entities are to be held responsible for ensuring all people have access to human rights. The essays show us that the notion of who is human has continued to remain dynamic, as it should be, in envisioning human rights. These essays also tell us how many hopes of the framers of UDHR have remained unfulfilled.

The pattern of the essays shows an overwhelming concern with human security. This concern reflects the state of the world where interstate conflicts have not lessoned, indeed the range of weapons has increased exponentially, so that people not only experience direct effects of war and conflict, but indirect ones including environmental degradation. In addition, inter-state conflicts have also increased substantially (Gledditisch *et al* 2002, or for an update see UCDP/PRIO 2009), as has asymmetric warfare (see Caforio, Kuemmel and Purkayastha 2008) so that more and more people are drawn into zones of conflict. While the popular perception tends to think of male soldiers and warfare, essays in this collection talk about the impact of conflict on children and women as well. Equally important, the authors of the essays reflect a conceptual trend by bringing concepts of food and well-being to the security discourse. As Mary Robinson (2005) has pointed out, while the world has focused on the 25,000 deaths due to terrorist violence especially from 2001, and directed billions of dollars for 'security', there were

250,000 deaths *each year* due to hunger, malnutrition, and preventable diseases. Further, just as the Nobel Peace prize committee awarded Wangari Mathai for her work on planting trees to restore war-torn areas, some of these essayists bring the issue of earthcare to the purview of a human rights framework. The authors dwell on the limits of some existing formal legal instruments, while emphasising the need for legal protections for non-heteronormative populations. Last, but not the least, they focus on human rights education, linking socialisation, cultural changes and the realisation of human rights.

This collection encapsulates hopes and critiques of young people from Armenia, Austria, Brazil, Cambodia, Costa Rica, Egypt, Italy, Kenya, Laos, Macedonia, Philippines, Uganda, UK, USA, and Venezuela – people who are passionately committed to, and are actively engaged in fostering a world where more people can access human rights. Thus, their essays, with their views on what needs to be addressed, and, how we should go about attending to these gaps, serve as an important marker of how far we have come in our struggle to realise human rights and how much further we have to travel on this road.

NOTE: I would like to thank Abhijit Mazumder for enthusiastically agreeing to publish this book. Amii Omara Otunnu has been a constant inspiration for showcasing how academics can still be passionately engaged in promoting human rights. Nana Amos is the bedrock of the UNESCO Chair for Global Human Rights office. Without her, the actual work of getting amazing people together, would never be complete. Sergio Mobilia, who now works at Google Argentina, as a senior analyst, shouldered the entire responsibility of putting these essays together. Along with members of my family – especially those who sacrificed much that others would have a better life – my thanks to these friends and colleagues.

REFERENCES

Armaline William, Glasberg Davita, and Purkayastha Bandana, 2011, *Human Rights in Our Own Backyard: Injustice and Resistence in the US*, University of Pennsylvania Press, Philadelphia

Caforio Giuseppe, Kuemmel Gerhard, and Purkayastha Bandana, (Ed) 2008, *Armed Conflict and Conflict Resolution: Sociological Perspectives*, Bingley, UK: Emerald Group

Cook Rebecca, (Ed) 1994, *Human Rights of Women: National and International Perspectives*, University of Pennsylvania Press, Philadelphia

Donnelly Jack, 2003, *Universal Human Rights in Theory and Practice*, (2E), Cornell University Press, Ithaca, New York

Ertürk Yakin, 2005, 'The UN Agenda for Women's Rights and Gender Equality', *Perceptions: Journal of International Affairs*, X (2): 91-113

Gleditsch Neil, Wallerstein P, Erikkson M, Sollenberg M, & Strand H, 2002, 'Armed Conflict 1946–2001: A New Dataset', in *Journal of Peace Research*, 39(5), 615-637

Glenn Evelyn Nakano, 2002, *Unequal Freedom: How Race and Gender Shape American Citizenship*, Harvard University Press, Cambridge, MA

Ishay Micheline, 2004, *The History of Human Rights: From Ancient Times to the Globalisation Era*, University of California Press, Berkeley, CA

Lauren Paul, 1998, *The international Evolution of Human Rights*, University of Pennsylvania Press, Philadelphia

Pearce Tola Olu, 2001, 'Human Rights and Sociology: Some Observations from Africa', *Social Problems* 48: 48-56

Purkayastha Bandana, (2008), *Building and Sustaining a Fabric of Peace: Notes from the Field* in Giuseppe Caforio, Gerhard Kümmel and Bandana Purkayastha (Ed), *Armed Conflict and Conflict Resolution: Sociological Perspectives*, Bingley, UK: Emerald Group, p.393-411

Robinson M, (2005), *Connecting Human Rights, Human Development and Human Security*, (p.308-316) in Wilson R, (Ed), *Human Rights in the War on Terror*, Cambridge University Press, Cambridge

Sardar Ziauddin, Nandy Ashis, Merryl Wyn Davies, and Claude Alvares, 1993, *The Blinded Eye: 500 Years of Christopher Columbus*, The Apex Press, New York, The Other India Press, Goa

Sen Amartya, 1998, 'Universal Truths: Human Rights and the Westernising Illusion', *Harvard International Review* http://findarticles.com/p/articles/mi_hb137/is_3_20/ai_n28713640/accessed on 26 July 2011.

UCDP/PRIO 2009 Armed conflict dataset. Available at: http://www.prio.no/CSCW/Datasets/Armed-Conflict/UCDP-PRIO/Armed-Conflicts-Version-X-2009/

Sixty Years of Relentless Human Rights Activism

A Youth Vindication of the Universal Declaration of Human Rights

Sergio Mobilia

Every time a human being is denied access to the fulfilment of his/her basic needs, disrespected, or subjected to unfair treatment based on certain personal or social characteristics, one or more of his/her "universal, interlinked, indivisible, and inalienable human rights" is/are being violated. Such human rights abuses and atrocities are often conceived of as the products of organised crime or authoritarian states. Yet, how often do we take a moment to reflect on the impact of our daily actions, social behaviour and life-guiding ideologies in terms of human rights violations? How often do we step back and consider the effects of our social assumptions and national legislation on our lives as well as on those of other people? And even when we do, how do we usually conceptualise 'other people'? Do we understand the experiences of others as human beings in their full capacities? Or do we tend to view them as individuals devoid of humanly need, expectations and feelings? In other words, how and when do we care about human suffering and human hope?

The concept of *human rights* has not had an uncontroversial history. After all, who gets to define who is human and what their rights (and wrongs) are at a certain point in time in a specific sociocultural context? Notwithstanding this philosophical conundrum, contemporary societies have managed to build on strong legacies of both respectful and abusive practices among members of the human family and to develop related bodies of legislation, declarations, covenants, treaties and other (non-)binding international legal documents for the regulation and safeguarding of human dignity and respect. One such major document is the *Universal Declaration of Human Rights* (1948), drafted by a visionary group of committed international leaders in the aftermath of World War II. The *UDHR* stated in writing for the first time in history what should be obvious to us all as human beings, yet something which history has shown is still not clear to every one of us in the world to this day: that each and every human being regardless of gender, race, ethnicity, socio-economic status, disability, sexual orientation, and/or faith is a rights-bearer simply by virtue of his/her humanity.

Sixty years after the signing of the *UDHR*, a new generation of likewise committed activists between the ages of 18 and 30 met at the *University of Connecticut* in Storrs, USA to renew the early visionaries' pledge to safeguard the human rights cause in a world increasingly torn by clashes of vested interests. Over eighty young human rights activists were recruited from among nine-hundred international applicants by a committee of world-renowned human rights leaders to participate in the *Fourth International Leadership Programme: A Global Intergenerational Forum* organised by the *UNESCO Chair & Institute of Comparative Human Rights* at the *University of Connecticut*, USA. For nine days in the month of August 2008, these human rights enthusiasts discussed the world's most pressing problems today – from poverty and health to food insecurity and the need to create a global culture of peace. The synergy developed by the group as a whole was beyond description: no words could accurately capture the sense of mutual empowerment and commitment towards the betterment of the international community that pervaded the Forum. The debates were heated; the resulting projects, many and fruitful. Among them is this book of selected essays by the world's new generation of human rights activists.

A UNIQUE PERSONAL EXPERIENCE

As a former coordinator of the UNESCO Chair *Student Ambassadors for Human Rights* Programme, I was humbled to be recruited by the Executive Director Dr Amii Omara-Otunnu to be part of the Forum's Planning and Application Committees. Little did I know at the time that, a few months later, post-graduate life's unexpected turns (as well as other people's missed flight connections) would land me the chance of interacting very closely with those eighty participants at the Forum in my double capacity as conference rapporteur and group facilitator? By the closing of the Forum, I was apprised of Dr Omara-Otunnu's wish to appoint me *Associate to the UNESCO Chair & Institute of Comparative Human Rights*. I am proud to say that this collection of essays is the result of the first of hopefully many more projects I intend to embark on with Dr Omara-Otunnu and his team in the years to come.

As editor-in-chief of this publication, I was offered the unique opportunity to work again with nineteen 2008 Forum participants from Africa, Asia, Europe and the Americas on a more personal basis: with each of them, we drafted and redrafted their essay with utmost care, picking and choosing every sentence, every word, and every comma. We worked ceaselessly over the 2009 New Year break and beyond. Each of us from our remote part of the world did our fair share to meet our common goal: the timely publication of this truly global book on human rights by the emerging leaders of the world. Needless to say, all unintended omissions and mistakes remain my sole responsibility.

The essay selection process was unusually challenging – the quality and number of submissions was not negligible, while the breadth and depth of the topics discussed were simply superb. Yet, each of the selected essays was chosen for its uniquely passionate discussion of a specific human rights issue in a specific social and cultural context, as well as for its hopeful outlook based on concrete action plans to redress the abuses under review. I strongly believe that this book challenges unfortunately widespread characterisations of youth as apathetic and inactive towards social injustices and human rights violations. In fact, *Human Rights: Voices of World's Young Activists* consists entirely of example after example of youth-led, action-based human rights activism. This collection stands as concrete evidence that there are many committed youths in the world not only willing to work for positive change in their contexts, but actually doing it on a daily basis.

ON CONTENT AND STRUCTURE

The contributions in this collection discuss a range of human rights issues that criss-cross in a diversity of regions and cultures around the world. Furthermore, they are representative of the variety of challenges identified in the United Nations' *Millennium Development Goals* (*MDGs*), aimed to reinforce the commitment spelled out in the *UDHR* to achieve the universal enjoyment of every human right by every human being, present and future.

The essays in this collection fall naturally into seven interrelated sections: Human Trafficking & Security; Children & Youth in Poverty or Conflict Zones; Environmentalism & Earthcare; Food Security & Health; On the Legal Protection of Non-Heteronormative Identities; The Use of Legal Instruments for Social Justice; and Human Rights Education. The topics are controversial; the authors' perspectives are passionately refreshing and clearly illuminating. In the following pages, the reader will be exposed to an impressive array of perspectives and issues. Arpine Kostanyan from Armenia discusses human trafficking, while Lindsay McNicholas from the USA links this issue to children's commercial sexual exploitation. To complement these two essays, Elena Mihajlova from Macedonia closes the section with an exploration of the concept of human security in post-conflict multicultural societies.

In the section on children and youth, in poverty or conflict zones, Awici Charles Churchill explores the issue of youth participation in post-conflict Northern Uganda. Additionally, Cambridge-based Anthropology student Amiya Bhatia discusses the impact of armed conflict and the transition to peace on Nepali children, while Phearun Kuch looks at the issue of street children in his native Cambodia. On an environmental note, Lina Mata Guido from Costa

Rica discusses youth participation and Earth-care, while Vannaphone Mina from Laos PDR delves into the issue of clean water sustainability.

The issue of food security is also a major concern for today's human rights movement. Thus, Dickens Molo from Kenya and Angelina Reif from Austria look at the right to food in light of the *MDGs*. From a health standpoint, medical doctor Andrea Labruto from Italy thoroughly discusses the use of the Internet to bring HIV/AIDS information to African populations, while Haksym Chhay from Cambodia writes about human rights and sexuality by advancing a critical review of *UDHR* Article 16 in light of the human right of homosexual people to legally marry and establish families.

From the legal quarters, two lawyers and an amazingly productive college senior look into the issue of legal instruments for social justice. Raquel Nunes of Brazil opens the section with her discussion of the use of the law as a tool for social change by analysing a case of land regularisation in a Brazilian slum. Additionally, Aheli Purkayastha of Pennsylvania, USA looks at restorative justice and the location of the individual in the *UDHR*, and Beatriz Borges Urrutia from Venezuela critically examines the potential of the *MDGs* as "the solution to the world's problems".

In my own experience as former coordinator of a *UNESCO* human rights education team, it seemed both natural and conceptually appropriate to close this book on challenges to human rights with the empowering hope of human rights teaching and learning. Thus, in the last section of *Human Rights: Voices of World's Young Activists*, the reader will find Nerina Maqueira from Argentina discussing education from a human rights perspective, while Nermine Mounir from Egypt delves into peace education as an empowering human rights tool. Moreover, Arcie Mallari describes his activist work in the field of education with children living in dumpsites in the Philippines. Finally, Sara Minkara, describes her school experiences in the USA in light of the widespread challenges in the Lebanese educational system. In view of the above, isn't it reassuring to know that these young men and women from around the world stand as the inspiring gatekeepers of humanity and its rights? There is no doubt that the ongoing actions of these young leaders in human rights represent ripples of hope that are already making the world a better place.

ACKNOWLEDGMENTS

As a concluding thought, I would like to express my most sincere thanks to the wonderful essay writers in this volume, who have worked diligently to meet the set deadlines with astonishing commitment and passion. It has been a tremendous pleasure to work with each one of them. I also wish to express my gratitude to the whole team at the *UNESCO Chair & Institute of Comparative Human Rights*, especially to Dr Amii Omara-Otunnu for his professionalism, his ardent passion for the cause, and for teaching me the ropes of 'practical idealism'. A special token of gratitude also goes to my dearest friends Faith Otunnu, Lena Dillman, Nana Amos, Kit Kort, Michelle Kort, Kamyar Momeni, Sudsiri Hemsri, Mehdi and Anahita Danesh Panah, Vanesa Pastormerlo, Adriana Vega, Micaela Epelbaum, Desirée Jaimovich, Kathy Tignor, Seth Nemeroff, Valentina Nicolova, Paula Ordonez Inda, Moeno Hotta, Xaé Alicia Reyes, Elizabeth Mahan, Bandana Purkayastha, Rebecca Williams, Nerina Maqueira, Cristina Banfi, Paula López Cano, Cristina Bardeci, María Graciela Abarca from the *Fulbright Commission Argentina*, Claudia Ferradas Moi, Susana Gullco and Enrique Groisman – wherever in the world we might be, we know that we can always count on one another.

Last but not the least, there are no words to express the depth of gratitude that I owe my wonderful family – my dear parents Eduardo Mobilia and Angela Amoroso, my grandparents, my brothers, their girlfriends, my cousins, and the whole crowd – for their support and patience during my 'work-visits' to Argentina over Christmas break. And, of course, to the two greatest inspirations in my life today: Camila y Matías Pastormerlo, my beloved God-children – thanks for making this world worth fighting for. I am positive that when you grow up, you will find an enhanced existence thanks to the work of our world's young human rights leaders!

Human Trafficking & Security

Human Rights and the Problem of Trafficking

Arpine Kostanyan

In 2008, we celebrated the 60th anniversary of the Universal Declaration of Human Rights. On 10 December 1948, the General Assembly of the United Nations adopted and proclaimed the *Universal Declaration of Human Rights* (*UDHR*), which, for the first time in history, codified universal human rights for all people in an individual context. The document was subsequently translated into more than 360 languages. It is very important for people to know that their human rights are protected. But first they need to be aware of the existence of the *UDHR* and of its functions.

WHAT DO PEOPLE KNOW ABOUT THE UDHR AFTER 60 YEARS OF ITS ADOPTION?

It is essential that human rights be protected by law. Every person is born with certain unalienable rights by virtue of their humanity. Although the UDHR was adopted sixty years ago, the rights of people continue to be severely violated in different regions of the world – one of the main reasons being that many people still have very poor knowledge of their rights. For instance, they may know that they have the basic right to be paid for the work they do, as well as the right to an education. However, there exist many other rights that many people are simply not aware of. The total number of human rights as spelled out in the UDHR is thirty. In my view, a key point of the UDHR is made in Article 2, which states that everyone is entitled to all the rights and freedoms regardless of race, colour, sex, language, religion, political or other opinion, nationality, social origin, property, birth or other status. Furthermore, no distinction is to be made on the basis of the political, jurisdictional or international status of the country or territory to which a person belongs, be it independent, trust, non-self-governing or under any other limitation of sovereignty.

When people are not fully aware of their rights, abuses can easily develop in the form of slavery, discrimination, and violation, among others. In this essay, I discuss one of the most severe forms of human rights violation: Human Trafficking. Human Trafficking is defined in the Preamble to the *Council of Europe Convention on Action against Trafficking in Human Beings* as "a violation of human rights and an offence to the dignity and the integrity of the human being and may result in slavery for victims" (Warsaw, 16 May 2005).

TOWARDS A DEFINITION OF HUMAN TRAFFICKING

What is trafficking of human beings? How many people in the world are aware of this problem? Unfortunately, the problem of human trafficking is quite large in scale, particularly in developing and/or Third World countries. Trafficking of women, for instance, has been addressed at the international, regional and national levels because many states are among victims' countries of origin, transit and destination.

Before the drafting of the *United Nations Protocol to Prevent, Suppress and Punish Trafficking in Persons* (October 2000), international treaties referred to trafficking without defining or clarifying, for instance, whether the crime included all forms of sex work. In that regard, Article 6 of the *Convention on the Elimination of All Forms of Discrimination against Women* states that "All Parties shall take all appropriate measures, including legislation, to suppress all forms of trafficking in women and exploitation of prostitution of women".

It is difficult to provide a definition of the word 'trafficking', given that there is little agreement in the international community as to how human trafficking should be defined. In early treaties, trafficking was often synonymous with the trade of women for prostitution purposes. Later on, the term also began to be used for the smuggling of male and/or female migrants over borders for economic gain. In the late 1990s, the *Organisation for Security and Cooperation in Europe* (*OSCE*) argued that, "despite divergent definitions (of the term), there is a growing agreement that the problem of 'trafficking in human beings' involves two key elements: recruitment/transport and forced labour or slavery-like practices. Moreover, most experts agree that trafficking should be defined as involving deception or coercion of some kind". In other words, human trafficking is a multi-dimensional issue that implies, first and foremost, human exploitation.

The United Nations' current definition of human trafficking is to be found in the *UN Protocol to Prevent, Suppress and Punish Trafficking in Persons*, especially in terms of women and children, adopted in the year 2000 in Palermo, Italy (*Palermo Protocol*, 2000). *The Palermo Protocol* complements the *UN Convention against Transnational Organised Crime*, situating human trafficking in the said paradigm. Furthermore, the *Council of Europe Convention* (Warsaw, 16 May 2005) defines trafficking of human beings as "the recruitment, transportation, harbouring or receipt of persons" by means of threat or use of force or other forms of coercion, abduction, fraud, deception, the abuse of power or of a position of vulnerability or the giving or receiving of payments or benefits to achieve the consent of a person having control over another person. Moreover, exploitation includes, at a minimum, the exploitation of the prostitution of others or other forms of sexual exploitation, forced labour or services, slavery or practices similar to slavery, servitude or the removal of organs. A victim is defined as any person who is subject to trafficking by any of the means specified in the Convention. The consent of a victim to the exploitation is irrelevant where any of the means set forth by the definition (coercion, fraud, deception . . .) have been used.

Moreover, Amnesty International has identified several common characteristics of trafficking which are useful to advocates working to address the problem. Women constitute a large proportion of the overall number of people trafficked that are transferred within or across national borders from their place of residence. The illicit movement of women takes place in the hands of 'traffickers', loosely defined as people profiting from organising, carrying out or otherwise facilitating the illicit transit of persons. The majority of women find themselves trapped in debt-bondage, servitude or slavery-like conditions as a result of being trafficked. One of the reasons ultimately driving trafficking in women is the demand for employment – be it 'voluntary' or 'coerced' – in the sex industry. Every woman trafficked for work in the sex industry is likely to be subjected to human rights abuses directly resulting from the trafficking situation. There is evidence that the smallest number of trafficking-related human rights abuses occurs at the women's places of habitual residence, for such abuses often commence at transit locations and become more prevalent at the final destination. Trafficking in women reaps huge financial profits for the traffickers. That is the reason why there has been an increase in international organised crime over the last few years.

TRAFFICKING AS A HUMAN RIGHTS VIOLATION

Besides *International Law*, other more general human rights norms are violated whenever people become victims to trafficking. The problem of human trafficking has become a major issue that affects all regions of the world. Each year, an increasing number of people (mostly women and children) fall victim to intra and international trafficking for the purposes of sexual and/or other types of exploitation. The phenomenon has already hit such unprecedented levels that it is now considered a modern version of the old slave trade. Human trafficking treats its victims as commodities to be bought and sold, to be put to forced labour – usually in sex industries.

A number of human rights violations may occur in the context of trafficking. For example, in trafficking cases, a number of civil and political rights may be violated. These include the right to personal liberty and autonomy, the right to bodily integrity, the right to freedom of movement and expression, the right to freedom from torture or other cruel or inhuman treatment, the right to freedom from discrimination, and the right to freedom from forced labour and slavery. Trafficking may also violate a person's social, cultural and economic rights, such as the rights to health, free access to education and information, and favourable working conditions (including just compensation and a reasonable number of working hours).

BEYOND BORDERS: INTERNATIONAL CIRCUITS OF HUMAN TRAFFICKING

Human trafficking has become such a worldwide phenomenon that it is no longer necessarily restricted within national borders. It affects most countries in the world through its links to organised crime. As a highly lucrative activity, human trafficking has to be fought just as vigorously as drug trafficking and money laundering. Indeed, according to some estimates (see sources below), trafficking in human beings is the third largest illicit profit-making venture in the world after the trafficking of weapons and drugs. According to the United Nations' statistics, for instance, traffickers smuggle nearly two million women and children beyond their national borders every year, grossing 7.5 billion US dollars in the process. These days, organised human trafficking is indeed one of the easiest, fastest and most successful ways of making money with minimum risk, as opposed to other types of illicit business. Every year, an increasing number of people fall victim of trafficking, mainly for sexual exploitation (43 per cent), but also as underpaid or illegal labour in farms, sweatshops and private households (32 per cent). The International Labour Organisation (ILO) estimates the number at over 2.45 million, most of them being women and children.

Due to its transnational nature, at some level trafficking impacts virtually every country. Organisations that research migration patterns and human trafficking classify countries as *source, transit*, or *destination*. Simply put, the country of origin of a trafficking victim (i.e., the country where traffickers recruit women and girls) is referred to as a source country. Traffickers frequently move their victims through intermediary countries, often for extended periods, where the latter may even be forced to work. These countries are known as transit countries. Traffickers choose transit countries based on their geographical location (near a border or a port), their weak border controls, the presence of corrupt immigration officials, or their affiliation with the organised crime groups that are involved in trafficking. Transit countries generally have access to the destination country, which are those that receive trafficking victims. Destination countries are generally economically prosperous as they must be capable of supporting the commercial sex industry brought in by the trafficking organisations.

Country classifications become complex as countries come to fit more and more categories simultaneously. Some may serve as transit countries along a trafficking route and may also receive trafficking victims as a final destination. The 'Protection Project', a legal human rights research institute based at John Hopkins University's School of Advanced International Studies in the US, has created a series of maps with trafficking routes that illustrate the trafficking patterns among source, transit and destination countries around the world today. It is crucial that source, transit and destination countries cooperate and develop joint strategies to combat trafficking. As phrased in the US Department of State's *Trafficking in Persons Report for 2002*, "Destination countries must work with transit and source countries to stem the flow of trafficking; source countries must work not only to prevent trafficking, but to help with the reintegration of trafficking victims back into their home societies" (*Trafficking in Persons Report*, 5 June 2002, *International Engagement*).

WHY WOMEN?

Traffickers primarily target women because they are disproportionately affected by poverty and discrimination, which restrict their access to employment, educational opportunities and other resources. That is the reason why it is oftentimes the most vulnerable layers of the society (such as children, women, immigrants, representatives of agricultural communities, orphans, and in general people with a lack of education) that become the victims of human trafficking. The roots of trafficking in my home country of Armenia, for instance, are the same as those in former USSR countries, which still have not managed to develop stable economies and where rates of unemployment, corruption and poverty are indeed very high.

In such and similar contexts, women may become victims of trafficking as they seek assistance to obtain employment, work permits, visas and other travel documents. Traffickers prey on women's vulnerable circumstances, luring them into crime networks through deceit and false promises of decent working conditions and fair pay.

HUMAN TRAFFICKING PREVENTION

Given that human trafficking represents a major international problem with multiple implications for societies . . . What can we do as an international community to prevent this phenomenon and make the world a better place to live in? I believe that preventive action against trafficking must first and foremost be carefully coordinated in order to be effective. Measures should be taken by authorities and activists who fight trafficking to establish or strengthen national co-ordination among different bodies responsible for preventing and combating trafficking in human beings. Developing information campaigns will be particularly useful in different countries, especially in villages and small cities where people are not so well informed about the plight of trafficking in the world. Awareness raising and education should be the pillars upon which the fight against international human trafficking should be built.

A number of International organisations have played a big role in combating the problem. Rising concern about trafficking in human beings has also prompted international agencies such as Interpol, the International Labour Organisation (ILO), the International Organisation for Migration and the Organisation for Security and Co-operation in Europe (OSCE) to take action, so that many non-governmental organisations are now working hard to help victims of human trafficking. Furthermore, information, awareness-raising and educational campaigns for persons vulnerable to trafficking should be complemented with actions aimed at discouraging 'consumers' of services provided by trafficked human beings. Border control and measures to ensure the validity of travel or identifying documents are also among the measures necessary to prevent human trafficking. Additionally, civil society – and in particular global youth – has an important role to play in regard to trafficking prevention and victim protection.

PENALTIES AND SANCTIONS FOR HUMAN TRAFFICKERS

A number of countries are fighting the problem of human trafficking seriously by imposing high sanctions and penalties on the perpetrators. For example, the *Canadian Immigration and Refugee Protection Act of 2001* recognises trafficking in persons as a criminal offence and sanctions it with a maximum penalty of $1,000,000 and/or life imprisonment. Unfortunately, the penalties and fight against trafficking are not taken as seriously in my country as they are in Canada. However, some promising changes have been made since 2003. The first piece of Armenian legislation to specifically outlaw human trafficking and provide criminal penalties went into effect in the summer of 2003. While there is no separate law about trafficking in Armenia, the new Article N132 was incorporated into the body of criminal legislation in April 2003. This article states that groups or individuals who act either as organisers or participants in trafficking, sexual harassment, prostitution, sexual abuse, slavery, use of human organs, kidnapping, and/or rape are to be punished by law with a 4 to 8-year term of imprisonment, or fined to the sum of the minimum salary multiplied by 300 to 500 times.

Nevertheless, it is difficult to provide exact figures of human trafficking victims. When people are hidden and deported, the situation not only represents a serious danger for the victims but also impedes law enforcement as they are unable to cooperate in the prosecution of the criminals involved in the trafficking. Therefore, the European Union and its national government members have recognised the need to grant victims of trafficking special protection because of their crucial role in the investigation and prosecution of trafficking cases. A number of European countries (including Belgium, Italy, the Netherlands and Spain) have all amended their domestic legislation to aid the reintegration of trafficking victims and to enable them to cooperate with authorities. The victims are granted residency permits as well as housing and medical assistance. Moreover, in the United States, the Victims of Trafficking and Violence Protection Act of 2000 created two new visa categories which do not confer immigrant status but allow victims of trafficking to remain in the US during criminal prosecution and to receive certain benefits and services. The T and U visas are discussed in more detail in the *Trafficking: Law and Policy* section of the Act.

FINAL WORDS

Human trafficking violates both international human rights standards and national immigration laws, and thus can only be prevented by the joint efforts and cooperation of global partnerships and civil societies. Human trafficking or modern slavery is a big tragedy not only for the person who was trafficked but for all humanity. Even though we are all unique and thus different, we are all equal in our human rights. All human beings are born free and equal in dignity and rights. They are endowed with reason and conscience and should act towards one another in a spirit of brotherhood (*UDHR*, Article 1). Everyone has the right to life, liberty and security of person (*UDHR*, Article 3). In the universality of human rights, we should, therefore, embrace the tragedy of one person as the tragedy of all humankind. That is what my colleagues and I do in our daily work to bring about positive change in the world. And, we all should remember that no one can take away our human rights (*UDHR*, Article 30), as they belong to us and were created to protect us.

The Commercial Sexual Exploitation of Children and Human Trafficking

The Importance of the Media

Lindsay McNicholas

The sexual exploitation of children is a practice that has plagued the world for centuries. Children have been exploited, sexually molested, and subjected to physical and psychological violence in virtually every historical period and society.[2] The practices of objectifying children have not subsided with the dawn of a new millennium. In fact, an estimated 10 million children are currently victims of sexual exploitation.[3] Children are bought, sold, trafficked and abused as objects for the sexual pleasure of some adults. The objectification of children is capitalised upon through the tourist industry, where children are marketed for people to 'use' on sexual holidays. They are exploited for the purposes of generating profits, of which the children themselves see very little – if any at all.

Article 1 of the *Universal Declaration of Human Rights* (*UDHR*) expresses the importance of freedom and equality. Likewise, Article 3 states the rights to "life, liberty and security of person".[4] Furthermore, Article 4 solidifies the illegality of human trafficking and the Commercial Sexual Exploitation of Children (CSEC) by stating that "no one shall be held in slavery or servitude; slavery and the slave trade shall be prohibited in all their forms".[5] As we review the *UDHR*, many articles that can be used to address the issues of human trafficking and CSEC in today's world become apparent. However, child exploitation continues to grow exponentially because of the money and power involved in the practice.

Over the past few years, the international community has become increasingly aware of and sensitive to cases of human trafficking and CSEC around the world thanks to extensive media reports on the brutality of the sex trade industry. In a way, the media capitalise on the 'sex sells' mentality, so crucial in sales and embedded in CSEC and human trafficking. At the same time, they expose important issues of human rights violations to the world. It is this exposure to issues that is most important when the media reports on brothels or trafficking rings, be they local, national or internationally run. As far as the children's lives are concerned, the more people who become aware of their circumstances, the more support for the efforts to end CSEC and human trafficking.

Media support and exposure can be an integral part in developing a successful campaign for change, which can put an end to the human rights violations against those held in situations of slavery or servitude. Not only the CSEC industry (where children are bought and sold), but also the human trafficking industry in general have gained significant international attention by law-makers, organisations and the media. Films, exposés and extensive investigations have been covered by many different media sources, from large screen films like *Trade* starring Kevin Kline (released in 2007) and made for TV movies like *Human Trafficking* with Donald Sutherland and Mira Sorvino (released in 2005), to popular news reports from *Anderson Cooper 360* on CNN. These reports and films, though sometimes through the use of fictional characters, portray the realities of human trafficking. When mainstream media sources deliver information regarding human rights violations to the masses, they are doing a service to society by providing their current and future support of world citizens to the movements striving to end atrocities towards children.

The hope is that widespread support of organisations and lawmakers working to end human trafficking and the exploitation of children will be generated through media outlets that spread the word of these violations. By circulating reports of human rights violations through mainstream media sources (in addition to less widely distributed material), I argue that public support will follow if people are provided with a source to direct their supportive energy. For example, organisations like *Free the Slaves* and *ECPAT International* (*End Child Prostitution, Child Pornography and Trafficking of Children for Sexual Purposes*) use media sources to raise awareness of the atrocities of human trafficking and the Commercial Sexual Exploitation of Children (CSEC). They provide information to political officials, local organisations, and the media in order to bring about change and awareness of the dangers involved in human trafficking. Through their campaigns for awareness, they encourage support for their initiatives through the donation of time and money by local, national, and international communities.

Organising social movements and raising global awareness in today's technology-driven age cannot be achieved without the support of the media. The anti-human trafficking movement, as well as organisations fighting against particular groups of traffickers (such as child traffickers) benefit from media involvement when the latter accurately portray the severity of this human rights violation. When TV news reports, films, and newspaper articles expose the truths and, more importantly, the widespread existence of human trafficking in our world, we can move forward towards prevention programmes and legal statutes with the goals of ending human trafficking.

The *Convention on the Rights of the Child* (1989) recognises that children need special safeguards because of their physical and mental level of maturity. Additionally, in recognising the difficult situations that some children live in, it is necessary to address their circumstances with special consideration. These considerations include the signing of agreements against the trafficking, sale, abuse, exploitation, and enslavement of children, since the latter are particularly vulnerable in societies around the world and should be protected from those seeking to take advantage of them.

As the media become involved in reporting this type of human rights violations, both financial and legal support can begin to make its way to organisations and legal frameworks working towards prevention and enforcement. Media campaigns targeted at potential child-sex tourists have been placed in airports, hotels, in-flight videos, magazines, taxi cabs, TV ads, billboards, and street signs around the world. Through media support and exposure, prevention and awareness-raising campaigns can be very successful. When movement organisers acknowledge the value behind media involvement, extensive support can develop.

If one looks at the organisation and development of other movements for change and awareness-raising (such as the domestic violence movement in the United States), it becomes apparent that both widespread knowledge of the issue and response for change are possible. Prior to the domestic violence movement gaining strength and eventually achieving success by creating household awareness of the term, the issue was viewed as a private matter that was not to be discussed in public. But today, after decades of fighting for support and the recognition of the immorality of domestic violence, it has become a commonly recognised issue that people understand as wrong and preventable by reporting to officials when faced with instances of abuse. Media involvement and strong voices from movements portray domestic violence victims in different modalities, which contribute to the widespread acknowledgement of the wrongful nature of abuse between partners.

The hope for the anti-human trafficking movement is to do just as the domestic violence movement did in creating household recognition of the issue—not only in the United States and Western nations, but also all over the world. Citizens of nations around the world are seeking change where they can feel confident in calling their local law enforcement officers when they see something suspicious that may resemble slavery, exploitation, or abuse. When people recognise that human trafficking and slavery are illegal practices that can occur right next door, they are more likely to begin to report such actions. By reporting suspicious behaviour involving slavery, citizens can play a key role in ending the human trafficking networks. The more knowledgeable people are about these issues, the more risky it becomes for human traffickers to successfully run their exploitive businesses. Through media campaigns and collaboration among organisations within the anti child-sex movement, public knowledge of the issue can be expanded, and higher prevention levels attained.

It is commendable when media sources portray or report on issues of human trafficking or CSEC—whether they be blockbuster films or local news reports. Regardless of the manner in which the message is communicated, when the world becomes aware that human rights violations are taking place, people will begin to promote change by demanding more of their local, national and international officials and encouraging them to truly invest in solutions for the end of human trafficking and CSEC. When those citizens believe in their hearts that wrongdoing is taking place, whether in a distant nation or in their neighbour's house, they can invoke their power for change on a national and international level.

When the media becomes involved in spreading awareness of these issues of human trafficking and CSEC (in which young children are forced into an industry that robs them of their childhood and lives), people feel empowered to create a movement of passionate and powerful voices for change. This is the change that could impact the lives of millions of people. Human trafficking and CSEC are human rights violations taking place in virtually every nation, making them issues that could consolidate a movement for change across borders. If people come together and unite around these human rights abuses, their international voice will have to be heard and addressed. This is a goal for international media sources to strive for when they are creating documentaries on all forms of human rights violations. This shows how the media can work in unison to end child suffering by inspiring the masses and encouraging global support for change.

REFERENCES

Brown Louise, 2000, *Sex Slaves*, Virago, London

'Child Wise', 2006, *Structural Causes of CSEC*, http://chilwise.net/causes-of-csec.php

ECPAT International, 2006, http://www.ecpat.net

O'Connell Davidson Julia, 2005, *Children in the Global Sex Trade*, Polity Press, Cambridge

The Universal Declaration of Human Rights, 1948, http://www.un.org/Overview/rights.html

Post-Conflict Multicultural Societies and the Concept of Human Security

Elena Mihajlova

In this essay, I discuss the concept of *human security*, and its importance and necessity in multicultural societies with high tension deriving from the cultural and identity disputes. There are many post-conflict multicultural societies (such as countries in the Balkan region) in need of a more comprehensive approach to the security and well-being of their citizens. 'Human security' is a concept that can be introduced in these societies as a powerful tool for guaranteeing their citizens' right to freedom and dignity.

THE CONCEPT OF HUMAN SECURITY

The concept of human security includes a shift of the focus (stress) from the state security to the security of people, obligations of the states to ensure security for their citizens, the interdependence of people and the fact that a lot of issues go beyond the state borders, acknowledgement of the importance of non-state actors, the request for accountability of violators of human rights and humanitarian law, and the most important: the recognition of the complexity of security issues and the need for multidimensional response.

Among the main threats to human security are military conflicts, crime, troubled transfers of governmental authority and so called 'unconventional' threats for the security, which spring from non-military activities of individuals and groups in society. Examples for this kind of threats are religious fundamentalism, violation of human rights, economic crises, and environmental changes. As the author Ramesh Thakur[6] describes: "Human security refers to quality of life of people in one society or state structure. Everything that degrades the quality of their life . . . is security threat."

The *1994 UNDP[7] Human Development Report* represents the first formalisation of the concept of *human security*, and thus the latter became associated to this document. In that year, the UNDP for Human Development introduced the term of 'human security', which includes seven dimensions: economic, food-related, health-related, environmental, personal, community-based and political. The seven dimensions of the UNDP concept of *human security* imply numerous potentially interconnecting and overlapping dimensions focused on human dignity (such as political, economic and democratic development; preventing the forced migration and absence of human rights; enjoying the political and cultural communities rights; maintaining the human environment; etc.).[8]

Until now the concept has managed to find its way into the foreign policies of some countries such as Canada, Norway and Japan who were among the first states to incorporate the concept of human security in their official foreign policies. It is also part of the UN framework[9] and the agenda of North Atlantic Treaty Organisation (NATO), and European inter-governmental organisations such as the Organisation for Security and Co-operation in Europe (OSCE), the Council of Europe and the European Union. For example (NATO) joins the wide approach to the security by recognising the importance of the political, economic, social and ecological factors.[10] OSCE comprehensive security concept focuses on the respect for human rights and fundamental freedoms, democracy and rule of law. For this organisation "strong democratic institutions and the rule of law play an important role in the prevention of occurring threats. Weak governments and the failure of the states to provide adequate and functional democratic institutions, which are able to promote democracy, can create a basis for series of threats".[11]

Yet, we must not ignore the fact that the incorporation of this concept onto intergovernmental organisations' agenda (although maybe not always registered under the label of human security concept) is happening simultaneously with the still influential positions according to which it is a concept without clear theoretical base, with barely sufficient political precedents, without consensual guiding definition, and extremely uncertain future. In this very gap, between its increased use as a possible powerful tool and a 'trendy' term criticised to bear the risk of meaning everything and nothing,[12] I will try to analyse it in the light of preventive diplomacy, especially important in the multicultural and post-conflict societies, allowing that the theoretical consensus will appear along the way through lengthy theoretical debate and political experimentation (for which again its application in these societies can be of a significant contribution).

HUMAN SECURITY AS A TOOL FOR PEACE IN POST-CONFLICT SOCIETIES

The human security offers a new point of view and wide pattern for evaluation of various policies. The systematic focus on the security of people is stressing the need for more concentrated attention on the key issues which the society is not addressing correctly yet. The measure (measuring) the welfare of all people, in the sense of their equal terms as human beings, is the main objective of the human security. This has a different effect on the multicultural societies: from one side goes beyond any geographical border and religious or ethnical differences and unites everybody in the global society; on the other side it focuses on each individual as a human being. These two factors are not mutually exclusive, but they both express the focus on the individual, today's human security trend. This stress put on the individuals, raises in them their solidarity as a feeling of belonging to the same group – the group of humans.

And further, the operational tools of the human security include practical indicators and initial values for each domain of the welfare.[13] The initial values play a key role in the risk(s) assessment in a society with cultural and identity problems. Going below those initial values (below that threshold), means poverty, which dangerously coincides with the different and often conflicting interest of the multicultural groups, and such combination can result in conflict. Since, the calculation of the human security level not only includes all minimal conditions for humanity, but also tries to calculate and prevent the sources of crisis.[14]

As we have mentioned above, the human security concept establishes a set of welfare areas, such as: democracy, political freedom, income, education, health. Their universality and essentiality reduces the scope of speculation against certain group, or within certain group. In other words, since the aforementioned areas cannot be commented on as unnecessary or irrelevant for certain cultures, the tendency to justify the internal restrictions in regard to their application on ethnical or religious basis is coming to its end. Although each aspect of the human security must be taken into consideration in order to maintain the balance while progressing, such balance can be yet fragile. In post-conflict situations, if the states are focused too much on consolidation of the political stability, they might be destabilised by the economical derogations (or any of the other factors). In many societies the transition was disturbed by the weak or negative growth, weak institutions, corruption and abrogation of social protection, leaving the people to wonder why the democratic forms of management are not offering the promised benefit.

Respect for the human rights is also an important segment in (and out of) the human security concept, without which it would remain empty. In the world today, there are numerous situations where different ethnical groups and different population groups end up in conflict because the fundamental rules in the society do not provide them decent and fair chances for life, or where one group within the society finds itself to be a victim of unfair treatment. Accordingly, the strategies for prevention of conflicts must be built together with the strategies for promotion and protection of human rights/minority rights, or liberal justice in combination with fair treatment of the cultural diversity (justice for the groups).

In our review, this introduces the issue of protection of minority rights, which is particularly complex in the multicultural societies. It deserves special attention because in the experience gained so far in building successful democracies, the cultural factors prove to be more important than economic ones. In these societies, contrary to the above mentioned, the unfounded optimistic expectations that the processes of modernisation and economic growth will replace, suppress or delete the ethnical and other cultural differences and identifications should be abandoned. There is a need for new, more subtle and more realistic development of strategy for building democracy with radical ethnic, religious and cultural differences and pluralism. Here the state has mainly the following obligations: accepting and respecting the universally recognised human rights and minority rights and incorporating them in an explicit manner into the internal legal order; assistance (by the state) in creating conditions in which people can realise their rights, especially the minorities members, which with the incentive measures of the state will be able to have equal treatment in enjoying the rights.[15]

FINAL WORDS

The intention of this text is to assess the content of the concept of 'human security' and all the possibilities that the concept is offering for the multicultural, especially post-conflict societies, as well as for other weak or fragile countries and countries in transition. It can be a powerful tool for guarantying the freedom from fear and the right to live in dignity. Such a connection can be identified through two important factors: firstly it is focused on the individuals and goes beyond every geographic, religious, traditional or cultural border. Secondly, such a stress in the entire society decreases the potentials for crises through different integration factors, such as: efficient democratic rule, respect of human rights, education. The application of 'human security' is clearly not the same thing as guaranteeing welfare in multicultural and post-conflict society. It is only a small step in the process of evaluation and alleviation of human suffering, yet a very important one.

REFERENCES

Annan Kofi, 2000, *Report of the Secretary-General on the Work of the Organisation, General Assembly Official Records* Fifty-fifth Session Supplement No.1 (A/55/1), New York, United Nations

Frckoski D Ljubomir, & Ivanov Gorge, 2003, *Contemporary Political Theories*, Forum, Skopje

Frckoski D Ljubomir, 2005, *International Human Rights Law*, Magor, Skopje

King Gary, Murray J L Christopher, 'Rethinking Human Security', in *Political Science Quarters*, Vol 116, N.4, 2001-2.

MacLean George, 1998, *The Changing Perception of Human Security; Coordinating National and Multilateral Responses; The United Nations and the New Security Agenda*, United Nations Association in Canada

McRae Grant Robert & Hubert Don, 2001, *Human Security and the New Diplomacy: Protecting People, Promoting Peace*, McQill-Queen's University Press, Montreal

Nef Jorge, 1999, *Human Security and Mutual Vulnerability: The Global Political Economy of Development and Underdevelopment*, 2nd Ed, International Development Centre, Ottawa

Owen Taylor, 2004, 'Human Security-Conflict, Critique and Consensus: Colloquium Remarks and a Proposal for a Threshold-Based Definition', *Security Dialogue*, Vol 35, no.3.

Ramcharan G Betrand, 2002, *Human Rights and Human Security*, Martinus Nijhoff, The Hague

Sadako Ogata, 1999, *Human Security a Refugee Perspective*, Keynote speech at the Ministerial Meeting on Human Security Issues of the 'Lysoen Process', Group of Governments. Bergen, Norway

Thakur Ramesh, 1997, *From National to Human Security, Asia-Pacific Security: The Economics-Politics Nexus*, Ed, Stuart Harris, and Andrew Mack, Allen & Unwin, Sydney

United Nations Development Programme (UNDP), 1994, *Human Development Report 1994*, Oxford University Press, New York, p.23

Children & Youth in Poverty or Conflict Zone

Youth Participation and Post-Conflict Recovery in Northern Uganda

Awici Charles Churchill

Since 2006, after the cessation of two decades of hostilities and armed conflict between the Government of Uganda and the Lord's Resistance Army (LRA) in Northern Uganda, the search for lasting solutions to the conflict has intensified. Several intervention strategies have been researched and discussed, yet little has been done to capture the involvement of young people in post-conflict recovery in order to restore peace and work towards rehabilitation and development. The vision of young people as leaders of tomorrow is contradictory to the reality of their upbringing (Baines, Stover & Wireda, 2005:21). In the words of Maria Montessori, "Those who want war prepare young people for war; but those who want peace have neglected young people and adolescents so that they are unable to organise them for peace" (Zovu, 2006:15).

The situation in Northern Uganda clearly demonstrates this aspect of the problem, where hundreds of children have been abducted and forced into child soldiering. Moreover, the resettlement of the formerly abducted and those affected by the conflict has since met with little success: the current intervention does not address the root causes of the challenge and was implemented without "a broad conception of the conflict and peace building that legitimises and encourages multiple roles relevant to different tasks in the progression of the conflict" (Lederach, 1995:23). Nevertheless, any intervention aimed at peace and development should gain a better understanding of the issues and their manifestations, and encourage young people to take an active role in rebuilding their lives and the future of their communities. I am in agreement with Mulako Mwanamwalye, former Chair, Commonwealth Youth Caucus, who remarked that, "I do not believe that the decision to involve the young can be postponed . . . perhaps the question to the older generation is: what do you plan to do without us" (Mokwena, N.d.:1).

This paper focuses on youth participation in post-conflict recovery in Northern Uganda. It begins with a short overview of the history of the conflict and its impact on young people, and goes on to outline a human rights framework for participation and its implications for social change and reform. Finally, it proposes possible solutions aimed at an active participation of young people for a peaceful and sustainable future in Uganda as a whole. Throughout this paper, the terms *youth* and *young people* are used interchangeably. Likewise, *participation* is used to mean a continuous process during which young people are involved in every stage of decisions, plans and resources that affect their lives (Checkkoway, N.d).

ARMED CONFLICT AND YOUNG PEOPLE IN UGANDA

Today, Africa is faced with one of the world's greatest violent conflicts – both intra and interstate. According to Zakiya, Morton and Vavra (2005),

> More than 50 per cent of the world's active violent internal and regional conflicts are in Africa. These conflicts have directly or indirectly affected over 75 per cent of the region's countries and populations, conscripted over 300,000 child soldiers, displaced over 30 million people, caused over one million deaths, destroyed social and economic infrastructure, damaged the environment, weakened institutions of governance, and generally impeded equitable sustainable development.
>
> (Synopsis section, para 1)

The history of Uganda has been marred with armed conflicts since its colonial era. Northern Uganda exemplifies the legacies of unaddressed conflicts and human rights violations which "produce cyclical patterns of violence in Uganda" (RLP, 2008:3). Northern Uganda has suffered from violent conflicts from the Karimojong cattle rustlers as long as the two have been neighbours, but the LRA rebellion has left the community even more vulnerable since 1986.

The last two decades of armed conflict between the Government of Uganda and the LRA forces has displaced almost the entire rural population, destroyed the region's infrastructure, killed a large number of innocent civilians, and turned many children into child soldiers. According to Chrobok and Akutu (2008:5), on the conflict in Northern Uganda, of the 50,000 to 70,000 people that have been abducted and used in hostilities, thousands of them are children. Moreover, there is no clear policy that specifically assesses the needs of young people and plans a strategy to address their challenges. Therefore, the young people continue to lag behind in community activities (*African Rights*, 2000:73).

The Peace, Recovery and Development Plan for Northern Uganda (*PRDP*), which runs from 2007 to 2010, does not explicitly offer comprehensive support to young people. There is, therefore, no clear linkage between the youth being leaders of tomorrow's society and their involvement and participation in peace and development activities (Baines, Stover & Wireda, 2005:21). Meanwhile, the signing of the Cessation of Hostilities between the Government of Uganda and the LRA in 2006 was a new beginning for the Internally Displaced Persons (IDPs), who are slowly returning to their original homes (UNDP, 2008:11).

This signing provides an opportunity for IDPs to return to their local communities and rebuild their lives and spaces. But the post-war peace-building process is likely to be complex and challenging due to the dependency syndrome developed among IDPs. Several interventions are primarily driven by international non-governmental organisations and governmental development agencies.

Peace-building approaches have, to a large extent, ignored the involvement and participation of young people. As the *USAID Report* (2004:2) notes, "there is a strong correlation between large youth cohorts and political [social, economic, cultural, and environmental] violence. When young people are uprooted, jobless, intolerant, alienated, and with few opportunities for positive engagement, they represent a ready pool of recruits for groups seeking to mobilise violence". In fact, the youth in Uganda are not only the primary victims of violence: they also face the problems of broken families, are victims of inefficient educational systems and unemployment, among others. This situation represents a breeding ground for potential future violence and unrest on a large scale. The exclusion of young people from a wide range of community activities (such as decision making, planning and the actual implementation of project initiatives) weakens the community base for peace and development. Social exclusion affects every level of their lives, including the political, social, economic, cultural and environmental dimensions. Ugandan youth have become mere observers of their fate.

According to Baines, Stover *et al* (2005), the young people in the northern provinces have grown up in conflict-ridden periods and have lost out in many aspects of life (including socio-economic, political and cultural rights) and are in turn constrained to contribute to public policies. Despite this terrible situation, the Government of Uganda is unable to meet the needs of the youths and has done little to ease their suffering. There are no youth-focused curricula that meet the challenges the latter face in this era of new technologies and globalisation. This lack of curricular resources continues to undermine youth involvement and participation in peaceful and sustainable community development.

Until now, education in Uganda has been used basically for job-seeking purpose other than those of maintaining social cohesion, ecological integrity and sustainable community development. Therefore, there is an urgent need to transform education in such a way as to reorient it towards the achievement of social purposes (Haaverlsrud, 1996). Through education, human beings should:

> be able to survive, to develop their full capacities, to live and work in dignity, to participate fully in development, to improve the quality of their lives, to make informed decisions,

> and to continue learning [. . .] The satisfaction of these needs empowers individuals in any society and confers upon them a responsibility to [. . .] further the cause of social justice [. . .] to be tolerant towards social, political and religious systems which differ from their own, ensuring that commonly acceptable humanistic values and human rights are upheld, and to work for international peace and solidarity in an interdependent world.
>
> (*The World Declaration on Education for All*, 1990:4)

I would, therefore, argue that youths need to be empowered for an effective contribution to peace and sustainable development in Uganda, where violent conflicts and underdevelopment have been occurring at an alarming rate. To build a stable society, we need to create the conditions for positive and constructive roles for youths in Uganda so that they will not have to resort to violence to satisfy their needs.

Education for empowerment should be redirected in such a way as to provide the youth with the necessary knowledge, skills and attitudes to help them think, act and react in a peaceful manner. Thus, young people will learn to actively participate in decision-making processes and bring about much-needed transformation in their communities. Should youths engage in peace-building and community initiatives, the stability and development of communities will only be enhanced. Hence, critical youth empowerment will bring about understanding and social progress in the process of community development.

THE RIGHT TO PARTICIPATION IN SOCIAL CHANGE

The right to participate is contained in the *United Nations Convention on the Rights of the Child* (*CRC*, 1989). This convention "provides a framework for the promotion of participation within a legal context" (Mokwena, N.d.:4). It recognises children and young people as "partners in the process of social change" and democratisation. Mokwena cites Marta Santos Pais of *UNICEF*, who explicitly captures this point:

> The Convention has provided a new vision of children. While acknowledging that [children and young people] are vulnerable human beings that require protection and assistance from the family, the society and the state (sic). The child is envisaged as a subject, who is able to form and express opinions, to intervene as a partner in the process of social change in the building of democracy . . . children [young people] can no longer be perceived as not-yet persons. (N.d: 4)

The vision of youth participation is widespread and has progressively been construed by the *Commonwealth Youth Programme* since 1980, and enshrined in the *Harare Declaration* (1989), which has informed discussions on several international forum (Mokwena, N.d.:1). The *Lisbon Declaration on Youth Policies and Programs* (*United Nations*, 1998), for example, states that "youth are a positive force in society and have enormous potential for contributing to the development and advancement of societies . . ." (Mokwena, N.d.:1). Mokwena further observes that "Youth participation is a double-sided agenda. It is put forward as part of a vision of a New World on the one hand and as a way of achieving that vision on the other". It is for that reason that "of the participation of youth is indispensable for a societal change and for deepening democracy. They are the leaders of tomorrow. They are not a problem to be solved, but problem solvers themselves" (Rudolph, H H 2000, in Merkle C, 2003:205; emphasis in the original).

ENHANCING YOUTH PARTICIPATION

As Burkey (1993) put it, "Participation is an essential part of human growth, that is development of self-confidence, pride, initiative, creativity, responsibility, cooperation, . . . this is whereby people learn to take charge of their lives and solve their own problems, is the essence of development" (in Mokwena, N.d.:2). Young people's involvement in the development of their societies requires a number of skills and abilities, and adopting certain attitudes and behaviour that are necessary for ensuring a better future (*World Summit on Sustainable Development*, 2002:3).

Active and sustainable youth participation is dependent upon well-founded systems and clear strategies. What Mokwena suggests is closing the gap with community development. Citing an example from an Australian community where young people's citizenship is undermined and clearly manifested in open discrimination against their looks, dress code and their ways of hanging out (even to the point of criminalising their activities), Mokwena (N.d.:7) includes the four possible solutions that research came up with to address the challenge, namely: developing stronger lobbies for young people among stakeholders and within community structures; recognising the role of local governments; institutionalising youth planning in local governments; and consulting with different sub-groups of young people on the design and planning of public spaces.

The situation in Northern Uganda is unique in that many young people have been abducted and most still remain in the bush. Others were born in LRA captivity and have suffered the gross violations of rights so often reported about the conflict. Today's Ugandan youth, the majority of whom were born during the conflict, have suffered from or been affected by the latter in one way or another, having lost out in a number of ways (Baines, Stover and Wireda, 2005). For example, the *Millennium Development Goals*, which embody the world's aspiration for human betterment as expressed in a limited set of numerical and time-bound targets (UNDP & UNICEF, 2000), cannot be achieved in the absence of peace, for no meaningful development can take place in such a context. Conflict aggravates hunger and poverty; disrupts education; increases gender disparity and child mortality; worsens maternal health; increases vulnerability for HIV/AIDS, malaria and other diseases; leads to environmental degradation; and further marginalises the disadvantaged.

The efforts to enhance youth participation should be accompanied by genuine reconciliation among local communities and integrated development initiatives necessary in addressing the underlying causes of the conflict in Northern Uganda. For a region that has been at war for two whole decades, the questions of militarisation and structural violence which deny people of their fundamental rights require special consideration. In particular, establishment of disarmament education should aim to create genuine awareness in people as to the negative impact of a gun culture on peace sustainability and development in the region. Additionally, it should empower the population to become more aware of the negative impact of militarisation and lobby the government to reduce military expenditure on arms, as well as criticising military solution to disputes, thereby encouraging peaceful conciliation of interest groups (Cawagas & Swee-Him, 1987). But this can only be achieved with a clear understanding of the issues at stake and their manifestations, and the willingness to address the root causes of the multi-dimensional problem. For, as Barash and Webel (2002) observe:

> No one – not even the most ardent advocate of disarmament – claims that doing away with weapons will solve the problem of war. So long as the underlying causes of personal, group, and state instability remain, and so long as human beings possess the capacity and inclination to resort to violence under certain circumstances, war will continue to haunt us. (p.315)

Moreover, as *The Hague Agenda for Peace* (cited in Reardon and Cabezudo, 2002:13) remarks: "In order to combat the culture of violence that pervades our society, the coming generation deserves a radically different education – one that does not glorify war but educates for peace, non-violence and international cooperation." Northern Uganda has certainly been plagued with violence for several decades and the present generation has been socialised into it. Therefore, there is blatant need to envision a peace education programme into the post-conflict recovery strategy for a peaceful and sustainable future. Education, as Sansivens (2001:131) puts it, is a vital system in the development of personal, social and cultural objectives. Formal and non-formal education, therefore, become means of leading society into new dynamics by which people can be exposed to alternative world views and ways of life.

Peace education requires a thoroughly-designed plan that promotes the values, attitudes and skills necessary to foster a culture of peace. This, in turn, calls on agents who will awaken and promote educational interest "as a driving force that will create new cultural and behavioural goals, new professions and occupations, new human dedications, new knowledge, new artistic manifestations and, finally, new prospects for the future" (Sansivens, 2001:131). Consequently, as the main social purpose of peace education is to eliminate social injustice, renounce violence, and abolish war, knowledge, skills and values need to be at the core of addressing challenges and creating opportunities for peace (Reardon and Cabezudo, 2002:18).

Virginia Floresca-Cawagas and Toh Swee-Him (1999) developed a holistic framework for peace education that responds to the multiple realities of people as experienced in the global South and North, as well as to the threats and consequences of violence in all its forms. This framework identifies six inter-related themes that underpin conflicts and violence. These include educating for dismantling a culture of war; educating for living with justice and compassion; educating for human rights and responsibilities; educating for intercultural solidarity; educating for environmental care; and educating for personal peace.

FINAL CONSIDERATIONS

This paper delved into youth participation in post-conflict Uganda. It explored various barriers to youth participation, among them social exclusion, the existence of broken families, inefficient educational systems, and unemployment and thus recommends that, in order to restore peace and development in Northern Uganda, appropriate peace education approaches are necessary. It recognises the need to build youth community capabilities through active participation, conflict resolution and ecological integrity. Youth participation in post-conflict recovery needs to be ensured but, first, challenges need to be identified and strategies and actions developed in order for young people to be fully able to take part in decision making in their communities. In doing so, young people in Uganda will finally be able to become full citizens who can responsibly and confidently contribute to building a peaceful and sustainable world.

REFERENCES

African Rights Working for Justice, (2000), *Northern Uganda: Justice in Conflict*, African Rights, London

Baines E, Stover E, & Wireda M, (2005), *War Affected Children and Youth in Northern Uganda: Towards a Brighter Future*, An Assessment Report, Retrieved on 27 January 2007 from http://www.macfound.org/atf/cf/%7BB0386CE3-8B29-41628098E466FB856794%7D/UGANDA_REPORT.PDF

Barash, D P, Webel, C, (2002), *Peace and Conflict Studies*, Sage Publications, London

Checkkoway, B, *Adult as allies*, Retrieved on 13 February 2007 from http://www.wkkf.org/pubs/YouthED/Pub564.pdf

Chrobok V, and A Akutu S, (2008), 'Coalition to Stop the Use of Child Soldiers' in *Returning Home Childrens perspective on Reintegration*

Education for All Forum, (1999), *Education in Situation of Emergency and Crisis, Educaion for All Assessment Thematic Study*, Emergency Educational Assistance Unit, Paris

Florencia-Virgina V & Toh S, (1999), 'Institutionalisation of Non-violence' in L Kurtz (Ed) *Encyclopedia of Violence, Peace and Conflict*, Academic Press, New York, Vol 2, p.211-222.

Haavelsrud, Magnus (1996), *Education in Development*, Ed, Arena, Tromso, Norway

Lederach J P, (1995), *Preparing for Peace: Conflict Transformation across Cultures*, Syracuse University Press, New York

Mokwena T, Youth Participation and Social Change-Lessons and Perspectives from Around the World, Retrieved on February 2007 from http://www.unoy.org/downloads/8302.pdf

Reardon B, & Cabezudo A, (2002) 'Teaching towards a Culture of Peace' in *Learning to abolish War*, Hague Appeal for Peace, NYC, USA

Refugee Law Project, (2008), *Conflict, Justice and Reconciliation in Teso: Obstacles and Opportunities*, Briefing Note No. 1, Kampala

Rudolph H H, (2000), In Merkle C, (2003), 'Youth participation in El Alto, Bolivia' in *Environment and Urbanisation*, Sage Publications, p.205-214, Retrieved on 13 February 2007 from http://eau.sagepub.com/cgi/content/abstract/15/1/205

Sansivens M A, (1990), 'Towards a Concept of the Educating City', in *The Educating City*, Printed by Barcelona Town Hall, Barcelona-Spain

The Hague Agenda for Peace and Justice, (1999), The Hague Agenda for Peace and Justice in the 21st Century, Retrieved on 6 April 2007 fromwww.haguepeace.org/resources/HagueAgendaPeace+Justice4The21stCentury.pdf

The Millennium Development Goals in Africa: Promises & Progress, prepared by UNDP and UNICEF at the request of the G-8 Personal Representatives for Africa, New York, June 2002

Toh S H, & Florencia-Cawagas V, (1987), *Peace Education: A framework for the Philippines*, Phoenix, Quezon City

Toh S H, (2004), 'Education for International Understanding towards a Culture of Peace: A Conceptual Framework' in V F Cawagas (Ed) *Education for International Understanding towards a Culture of Peace: Teachers Resource Book*, p.7-22, Asia- Pacific Centre of Education for International Understanding, South Korea, Seoul

UNDP (2008), *Returning to Uncertainty? Addressing Vulnerabilities in Northern Uganda*

Universal Declaration of Human Rights Document, 1948

USAID Office of Conflict Management and Mitigation, (2004), *Youth and Conflict: A Toolkit for Intervention*, United States Agency for International Development (USAID), Washington DC

Verhey B, (2001), *Child Soldiers: Preventing, Demobilising and Reintegrating*, Africa Region Working Paper Series No. 23, the World Bank Group, Washington, DC, Retrieved on 13 February 2007 from http://www.worldbank.org/afr/wps/index.htm

World Summit on Sustainable Development, (2002), Priorities and Initiative for Partnerships in Sustainable Development, Youth Major Group Declaration

Zakiya A, Morton A, & Vavra J, (2005), *Gender and Conflict in Africa: Research Presentation on Best Practices, Resources and Lessons Learned*, Retrieved on 9 February 2007 from http://www.usaid.gov/policy/cdie/session8-30.htm

Zovu B K, (2006), *Women's Peace Education: The Way to Reduced Structural and Cultural Violence in Kenya*, Thesis presented to the Europe

University Centre for Peace Studies. Austria, Retrieved on 29 December 2008 from
http://74.125.47.132/search?q=cache:TEVvq5T2lq4J:
www.aspr.ac.at/epu/research Nzovu.pdf+Those+who+want+
war+prepare+young+people+for+war%3B+but+those+who+
want+peace+have+neglected+young+people+and+adolescents+
so+that+they+are+unable+to+organize+them+for+peace&
hl=en&ct=clnk&cd=4

State of Peace, Promises for Nepal's Children

An Examination of the Impact of Armed Conflict and the Transition to Peace on Nepal's Children

Amiya Bhatia

Twelve years of conflict in Nepal between the Maoists[16] and the state security forces[17] have led to the deaths of over 13,000 people and affected thousands of children. The use and abuse of children in conflict violated the *Universal Declaration of Human Rights* (*UDHR*), the *Convention on the Rights of the Child* (*CRC*) and almost every international convention Nepal has signed and ratified to this day. The cessation of conflict in April 2006 did not mean immediate peace, nor did it signify that treaties and conventions – once brushed aside – would suddenly be collectively honoured. This paper uses a human rights framework to examine the role of children in armed conflict and in the subsequent peace process in Nepal and to raise questions about the politics and complexities inherent in implementing and using the *UDHR* in the often blurry transition between conflict and peace.

Firstly, in a context of change and continuing instability in Nepal, the collaboration of the new state, local NGOs, the UN, INGOs and, most importantly, children are crucial in order to discuss programmes and solutions which have been implemented to address the use of boys and girls in armed conflict and the subsequent challenge of their reintegration. Secondly, the events and lessons from Nepal can be used to raise questions about the larger issue of children in armed conflict, examine the tension between local and international legislation and investigate the discourses of accountability and the politics of safeguarding and protecting the rights of the child.

THE LOCAL AND THE GLOBAL

Despite an international and legislative framework, the global use of children in armed conflict has increased. Liberia, Sierra Leone and Sri Lanka are salient examples of conflict-affected states in which children are being recruited by armed groups. Today, according to the Special Representative for Children and Armed Conflict, there are eighteen 'situations of concern' around the globe, each one unique and with its own set of methodological trials. It has been estimated that over two million children have been killed in armed conflicts, and another six million have been rendered permanently disabled. Furthermore, over 250,000 children continue to be exploited as child soldiers[18] in today's world. A comparative analysis allows us to locate the situation in Nepal within a global context and build bridges between the experiences of children in different world conflicts, while respecting the local and individual nature of each context of conflict. This approach creates an arena where the local and global are forced to interact and where the sharing of policy ideas, youth responses and experiences provide not only strong cross-fertilisation of ideas, but also a depth of understanding and a powerful sense of solidarity.

A Human Rights Framework; Lost Childhoods & the Politics of the udhr

> "These documents are for diplomatic people, they are just ink on paper."
>
> (Young Man, 15, Liberia; *Will you Listen; Youth Report*, Companion to the 10-year *Machel Strategic Review*)

'Will You Listen' was an international effort by *UNICEF, UNFPA* and NGO partners to bring the voices of children affected by conflict into the arena of policy and law; the report highlights the importance of relevant declarations and conventions effectively addressing the realities of children associated with armed forces and armed groups in Nepal. It is imperative that "These documents" are not solely seen as "ink on paper" or for "diplomatic people", but rather for the children whose rights they are written, signed and ratified to protect and uphold. Revealing such chasms between policy and practice allow us as youth, policymakers and/or governments to rethink the scope, applicability and value of the declarations we hold to such importance, and to address the often conflicting roles played by individuals, governments and NGOs in interpreting, writing and implementing legislation.

The *Optional Protocol* to the CRC on the involvement of children in armed conflict (2002) sets 18 as the minimum age for compulsory recruitment or direct participation in hostilities,[19] whereas *Protocol II to the Geneva Conventions* of 1949, which is applicable to civil wars, sets the minimum recruitment age at 15. However, the Maoists recruited boys (and girls in fewer numbers) mostly between the ages of 10 and 16 into the militia, initially on a part-time basis to serve as cooks, spies, musical band members and messengers. Minors over 16 could officially join the *Peoples Liberation Army* (*PLA*) – although younger children often did so too – and were usually deployed away from home. Despite the somewhat disputed definition of a child presented here, the direct or indirect participation of children in conflict is identified as a war crime in the *Rome Statute for the International Criminal Court* (1998).

However, these conventions, together with the *UDHR*, were not only breached by the Maoists, but also by the state security forces. For example, the use and abuse of Article 3 of the *UDHR*, which states "Everyone has the right to life, liberty and security of person" is a salient example of how liberty and security have varying definitions – thus making it difficult to transpose international legislation onto the actions of involved parties. The Maoists unequivocally and repeatedly violated Article 3 of the *UDHR;* the right to life as well as the liberty and security of children and their families were disregarded. The use of a 'one family, one child' policy in parts of Nepal meant each family was threatened until they provided the Maoists a recruit for the PLA. Other recruitment strategies involved kidnapping as well as large rallies and propaganda campaigns, especially in schools. If not recruited or abducted, many children were displaced,[20] had to flee from Maoist threats or were otherwise undeniably affected by the toll the conflict took on their education, their families and their futures.

The ideals of liberty and security of person as enshrined in *UDHR* Article 3 merit further investigation. Many dalits[21] joined the Maoists to escape the marginalisation they faced under the caste system, and some girls enrolled in the cadres to protect themselves from abuse by the security forces. Although some children may have subscribed to the political vision the Maoists painted, millions of children in Nepal are engaged in work contrary to the *ILO Convention 182 (1999)* and therefore, economic incentives offered by Maoists for joining their forces were popular. Thus, joining the Maoists was, in several cases, a way for many to protect themselves and their families, and to earn a wage. This further complicates the implications and interpretations of Article 3, as joining the Maoists seemed for some a way to ensure 'security of person' and 'liberty' – debatably at a high cost to their personal safety. Although 'voluntary' enlistment, according to international legislation, remains illegal, the Nepali state and its security forces did not initiate a plan to encourage children to leave the Maoist forces. In addition, the lack of a juvenile justice system in Nepal meant that children who either surrendered to the security forces or were captured were treated like adults. In other words, they were often tortured and illegally detained, tried under anti-terrorist legislation, and terrified to leave the Maoists for fear of further and continuing persecution by the security forces.

As part of the ceasefire in April 2006, parties to the conflict agreed to prohibit the recruitment of minors, forbid sexual violence against women, and the Maoists stressed their willingness to abide by the *UDHR*, the *CRC* and the *Geneva Convention*. However, *Security*

Council Resolution 1612 (adopted in its 5235th meeting held on 26 July 2005) implemented a monitoring and reporting mechanism on violations against children in armed conflict in Nepal which proceeded to find approximately 1,576 children were recruited after the ceasefire. Furthermore, Pushpa Kamal Dahal, the leader of the Maoist party, told *Human Rights Watch* that the only children in the PLA were those who had lost parents in the conflict and who were unable to care for themselves. Dahal thus portrayed the Maoists as safeguarding the security of these children and granting them the rights that *UDHR* Article 3 upholds.[22]

Subsequently, the Maoists continued to publicly deny the employment of children and have failed to formally release child combatants from cantonments,[23] denying them access to the benefits of the peace agreement. Legislation and a human rights perspective were, therefore, used to different ends by the Maoists, the state and by the UN leaving little common understanding of how children who have been victims and perpetrators of conflict must be treated. Since peace does not solely mean the cessation of conflict, the current challenge is to continue to bridge the gap between policy and practice by extrapolating the promised peace from the signed agreement to the cantonments, the communities children once called home, and to lobby the state to incorporate a series of legislative commitments in the process of Constitution writing.

LOOKING AHEAD: REINTEGRATION AND THE PROMISE OF A NEW STATE

After a process of disarmament and demobilisation conducted by the United Nations Mission in Nepal (UNMIN) as well as other NGOs and UN organisations, the reintegration of boys and girls affected by the conflict remains a daunting and challenging task.[24] Partly as a result of international concern at the lack of urgency by Nepal's government to formally release children, despite formally signing a peace agreement, Radhika Coomaraswamy, Special Representative of the Secretary-General for Children and Armed Conflict visited Nepal in December 2008, after which Pushpa

Kamal Dahal agreed to formally release 3,000 children[25] from the cantonments. The *Optional Protocol to the CRC* requires that the government take "all appropriate measures" to promote the physical and psychological recovery as well as social reintegration of children who have been victims of the armed conflict. This duty is reiterated in the *Paris Principles*, which provide detailed guidelines on reintegration. A *Joint Declaration* was signed in March 2008 by the Maoists and the other political parties in which they promised the state would "allocate resources to the maximum extent possible to meet the basic needs and fulfil the rights of children". Post-elections,[26] the Maoists emerged as the largest party in parliament and are now collectively responsible for restoring the social and political rights their own party once violated.

The UN, NGOs, civil society and children must continue to play a role not only in influencing policy and lobbying the government, but also by creating awareness about the situation of children in armed conflict and during the transition to peace. Child Workers in Nepal (CWIN) started the *Children as Zones of Peace Campaign* in 2003, which gives centrality to child participation in building a national coalition against the violation of child rights and which strives to in. *UNICEF's Program for the Reintegration of Children Associated with Armed Forces and Armed Groups* (*CAAFAG*) in Nepal advocates and facilitates the release, return and care of children associated with armed conflict, and runs capacity building sessions for NGOs, community groups and civil society; programmes in 34 district offer education, vocational training, and psycho-social support for children through.

Both these initiatives stress the need of a long-term emergency response and hold child participation in the peace process as crucial to their aims. *CWIN* has used creative approaches like art, poetry and music for children affected by the conflict to share their experiences. Such campaigns merit greater youth and community support, as they ensure that the history of human rights violations and individual experiences of children are not forgotten or denied by those in power. "Will you Listen" is an excellent example of this approach as it embodies an international effort to bring children into the mainstream decision-making process.

When seeking solutions, it is important to recognise that the needs of children are not all the same, but vary with location, the role they played in the conflict, gender, age and ethnicity, among others. Offering the same basic support is useful and non-discriminatory. However, different needs are required to be further addressed at the state and at local levels; in Kathmandu, for instance, it is important to protect children from recruitment by the Youth Communist League (YCL),[27] which has been criticised for its excessive violence and intimidation techniques. There is urgent need for counselling to help youth negotiate entry into schools or night schools, and for income-generation programs. Supporting children to make informed decisions about whether and how to return home is crucial, as is the identification of possible sources of support at home.

Girls in particular face challenges in reintegration – especially those who are now pregnant, or have a child and may face stigmatisation in their local communities. Children born during the conflict need to be registered with the state, highlighting a pre-existing problem of birth registration, and girls who are mothers have special health and social needs. For older youth, there are few economic opportunities in rural Nepal so many may prefer to stay in urban areas. This returns to the ideas of liberty and security as iterated in Article 3, as it is problematic to assume that sending children home (after several years in some cases) is the safest and simplest solution; instead, it may be but a step to granting children the rights that were seized from them and one which may not eradicate threats of re-recruitment, for example, in the conflict in the Terai region of Southern Nepal.

The role of youth in 'New Nepal' comes against a backdrop of changing social and political processes, as well as economic uncertainty and is undeniably more important than ever before as Nepal forges its path from conflict to peace, from Monarchy to Republic and from Hindu to secular. Whether it is political activism, awareness campaigns through the use of local radio programmes, street theatre, or creating a model child-friendly Constitution, youth will continue to play a role in influencing public opinion and ensuring their voices and rights are incorporated into the Constitution-writing process. This process should not escape the attention of the government, media and international community and will be directly relevant to the future of the thousands of children whose lives have been affected in conflict by creating a culture in which the rights of child receive priority.

Thus, the role of the new state-in-the-making seems to be to share information with the UN and other organisations, commit to signed declarations and to supporting the *National Plan of Action*.[28] Most importantly, Nepal's new Constitution must be child-friendly; the Constituent Assembly is now under pressure to create a framework for a juvenile justice system and ensure the effective accountability for violations and abuses committed against children during armed conflict.[29]

SIXTY YEARS OF INSTITUTIONALISED HUMAN RIGHTS

To conclude, the *UDHR* represented a global step to enshrine values, inalienable rights and a hope that the ideals of human rights would transcend territory and politics. Thus, in one joint declaration in 1948, our understanding of rights and the development of the future were definitively transformed. Yet it quickly became evident that values are relative and inalienable rights are discarded in the pursuit of territorial expansion and political agendas. Although the *UDHR* is a document that is quickly evoked today in the defence of children, this declaration is neither binding, nor really universal. However, sixty years from its inception, the *UDHR* remains an idealistic and useful tool to attempt to evaluate and measure the well-being, freedom and security of human beings.

This process can never be flawless, yet it provides a framework within which to reconcile, or transcend, dichotomies like the relative and the universal, and examine the interplay between local voices and international legislation. However, interpretations of liberty, security and what designates freedom – coupled with a disputed legal definition of what a child is – make agreement on policies increasingly challenging. Children are politicised in the process and in an urge to redefine roles and fulfil legislation, the complexities embedded in ideas of choice and liberty must not be dismissed. It is imperative that Nepal as a nation creates consensus on the urgency to guarantee life, liberty and security for children affected by the conflict, who have already paid a high price for peace – not perhaps with their present lives, but with their futures. Doing less than this would erode the goals of the Maoists to create a new state based on the principles of equity, dignity and social justice.

REFERENCES

Cowan K, Dembour M & Wilson R A, 2007, *Culture and Rights*, Cambridge University Press, Cambridge

Wilson A, 1997, *Human Rights, Culture & Context*, Pluto Press, London

Coalition to Stop the Use of Child Soldiers, 2008, *Child Soldiers Global Report*

Children in the Ranks: The Maoists Use of Child Soldiers in Nepal in *Human Rights Watch (2007)*

UNICEF, 2008, *Programme for the Reintegration of Children Associated with Armed Forces and Armed Groups in Nepal; Evaluation Report*

Child Workers in Nepal (CWIN), http://www.cwin.org.np

Together for the Betterment of Street Children

Phearun Kuch

Childhood is a life stage in which every developing person requires the guidance and comfort of a caring family and the formal education provided by schools and other institutions in order to develop into full citizens who will eventually contribute to the process of nation- and world-building. Unfortunately, these rights are seldom accessible to street children, whose numbers keep increasing all over the world. The United Nations estimated that the worldwide street children population (i.e., 3- to 18-year-old) in 2001 was of 150 million, and rising on a daily basis. Approximately, 40 per cent of these children were homeless and the other 60 per cent worked on the streets to support their families.

In Cambodia, street children are categorised into three groups as per the official classification: (1) street-living children, i.e. children who have completely cut off their ties with their families, or have no family and have, therefore, made streets their home; (2) street-working children, i.e. children who spend all or most of their time working on the streets to provide an income for their families or for themselves, but return home regularly or irregularly; (3) children of street-living families, i.e. children who live with their families on the street. In Phnom Penh, the capital of Cambodia, alone, there are about 1,800 street-living children, 10,000 to 20,000 street-working children, and approximately 20,000 street-living families (*National OVC Task Force*, 2007).

Very often, these children are at high risk on the streets: they face sexual and physical abuse, gang involvement, child labour, drug use, food shortage, and health problems. They have no chance to meet their basic rights as established in the *Convention on the Rights of the Child* (1985). Furthermore, street children are denied – among other – the rights to dignity (Article 1), security of person (Article 3) and education (Article 26) as spelled out in the *Universal Declaration of Human Rights* (*UDHR*).

STREET CHILDREN IN CAMBODIA

The issue of street children is serious in Cambodia, a post-war developing country. To respond to this social problem, *Friends-International* (an organisation that works with marginalised urban children and youth, their families and their communities to build better futures for them) has been taking concrete actions in cooperation with local governmental bodies, the business sector, and individuals from different community levels. For instance, projects such as the *Street Children Network*, *ChildSafe Network*, and *Home-Based Production* have been established and implemented since 1994 to effectively help street children improve their lives off the streets. These projects entail three dimensions: Development & Integration, Prevention and Protection.

a. Development & Integration:
The Street Children Network Project

Mith Samlanh, a *Street Children Network Project* member, works to develop, integrate and protect street children from all forms of risk on the streets. Project members work to respond to the immediate needs of street kids in accordance with the *Convention on the Rights of the Child* (*CRC*). With this objective in mind, Mith Samlanh coordinates various teams and sub-projects working in two types of sites – in-centre and out-centre. For instance, as for out-centre activities, *Medical Outreach Teams* go on the streets to assist street children and street families, while *Life Skills Outreach Teams* work to educate street children and other target groups about issues such as HIV/AIDS and STDs (i.e. Sexually-Transmitted Diseases). Furthermore, *Drug Outreach Teams* go on the streets to educate street residents in drug use prevention. All these *Outreach Teams* encourage street children to join the in-centre activities: they work closely with *Placement Teams* to get children into the Centre and assist them for their social reintegration into public schools, their families, and the world of employment. Likewise, those who are too old and do not wish to get an education can go to vocational training to develop skills in mechanics, electronics, welding, sewing, cooking, beauty salon, or laundry. During their study at the centre, children of both groups have chance to go for art and cultural activities, and to secure shelter, nutritional food, and medical care for themselves.

b. Prevention: The Home-Based Production Project

Home-based Production Team works to train street families in the city of Phnom Penh and other provinces to manufacture creative products to be sold in retail outlets for income generation. Likewise, the children in those families are encouraged to go to school instead of working on the street or migrating from the province. According to the *Friends-International Annual Report* 2007, the project has been highly successful. More and more families are participating in the project (55 families from poor communities and parents of former street children in Phnom Penh, and 13 families from Kampong Cham – a province in Northeast of Phnom Penh believed to be experiencing high work-related youth migration). According to the report, a total of 222 children benefited from this project in year 2007.

The following is the story of a family of former street children whose parents have participated in the *Home-Based Production Project*. This story was extracted from the Project's product catalogue:

Sokpha is the mother of 5 children, living in a community in Phnom Penh. Over the years, all her children have been supported by Mith Samlanh to stop working on the streets and are now attending public school and vocational training. Last year, her eldest daughter was placed in employment and is now working as a dressmaker in a Phnom Penh shop.

Sokpha has been participating in the home-based project since its inception. Her husband, who lost his legs after stepping on a landmine, has also recently decided to stop begging and is now producing great small cars made of recycled tin cans. The family now manages to make a regular and decent income from selling these products and their children are no longer placed at risk working on the street. (Original in English, p.18)

c. Protection: The ChildSafe Network Project

The ChildSafe Network aims at protecting children from all forms of abuse and exploitation (such as physical abuse, sexual abuse and trafficking) through the concerted efforts of individuals, private and public sector entities and the local government. Members of *The ChildSafe Network* include motor taxi and Tuk Tuk[30] drivers, and personnel from guest houses, hotels, internet cafés, restaurants, and tour agencies. Members are thoroughly trained to identify children at risk and report to the *ChildSafe* hotline manager when they see a child in a dangerous situation. The *ChildSafe* hotline manager will then contact the corresponding governmental authority.

As part of their campaign, the *ChildSafe* team has developed seven tips for tourists to Cambodia, particularly to Phnom Penh. One of them warns tourists to travel 'with eyes wide open'. No matter who we are or where we are from, each and every one of us has a chance to help children from all forms of abuse. The *ChildSafe* team has proposed a powerful motto for everybody to remember: 'Together, protecting children'.

FRIENDS-INTERNATIONAL FOR THE BETTERMENT OF STREET CHILDREN'S LIVES

Each one of us has a role to play in shaping up this world for the betterment of street children. At *Friends-International,* we believe in working together for a brighter future for the children of the world. At our head office in Phnom Penh, Cambodia and with an international team from France, the United States, Germany, Australia and Cambodia, I work as an IT/Designer in the office of IT/Production. I work with my production team and other teams to develop educational materials for street children and society at large. At *Friends-International,* we believe that, if we all work together as a team, we will make it happen. As former United Nations Secretary-General Kofi Annan, we adhere to the view that:

> When you see something that is wrong, no matter how big the problem is, ask yourself: Who else would like to change this? How can we work together? Take action with others who share your conviction. Have the courage to believe you can make a difference. As with everything in life, small steps count. If something has not been done before, it does not mean it can't be done; it only means you could be the first to do it.[31]

THE CYTI NETWORK: HELP US EXPAND IT!

The CYTI Network, which stands for 'with Children and Youth, we Transform and Innovate', is a worldwide network of organisations that provide the highest standards of services to marginalised urban children and youth (including street children and youth), their families and their communities. *The CYTI Network* was initiated by *Friends-International* to promote collaborative work among organisations from different parts of the world. The objectives of the Network are to: (1) PROTECT urban children and youth from all forms of abuse within the scope of the *International Convention of the Rights of the Child* (1985); (2) REINTEGRATE marginalised urban children and youth so they become actively involved in the development of their society; (3) PREVENT marginalised urban children and youth from engaging in risky behaviour and/or dangerous situations that compromise their futures; (4) IMPROVE the way the organisation works by promoting innovative and effective approaches with the active participation of the children and youth.

All member organisations of *The CYTI Network* are part of an active network which facilitates the sharing of the best practices, experiences and tools (e.g. *Street Children, ChildSafe,* Drug, HIV/AIDS prevention programmes, among others). Network members develop collaborative actions around the world, and receive important support and training from *Friends-International* to develop their own projects in terms of services, administration, marketing and/or finances. We are currently looking for international partners . . . so how would you like to join the CYTI Network?

REFERENCES

Friends-International Annual Report 2006
Friends-International Annual Report 2007
Friends-International Street Children Profile 2006
Friends-International Street Children Profile 2006
http://www.friends-international.org
http://www.childsafe-international.org
http://www.streetfriends.org
http://www.un.org

Environmentalism and Earth-care

Political Participation, Youth and the Environment:

Towards a Healthy Planet

Lina Mata Guido

> Tierra fresca y mojada,
> tierra seca y ardiendo,
> te he de llevar amada,
> te he de llevar sufriendo.
>
> Jorge Debravo (*Tu, la Tierra*)[32]

2008 celebrates sixty years of the official recognition of universal human rights in a written document – the first universal statement on the basic principles of inalienable human rights, and a common standard of achievement for all peoples and all nations.[33] Said document is the *Universal Declaration of Human Rights* (*UDHR*), adopted by the United Nations General Assembly in 1948. The *UDHR* lists a variety of basic rights and freedoms, including the right for all citizens to participate in the political process of a country:

> Everyone has the right to take part in the government of his country, directly or through freely chosen representatives. Everyone has the right to equal access to public service in his country. The will of the people shall be the basis of the

> authority of the government; this shall be expressed in periodic and genuine elections which shall be by universal and equal suffrage and shall be held by secret vote or by equivalent free voting procedures (Article 21).

In short, Article 21 of the *UDHR* declares the right to political participation.[34] This right can be understood from many perspectives, for example, as the right to vote in elections, the right to join a political party, or the right to be represented in parliaments.

In the following discussion, I link the right to political participation with environmental issues. First, I discuss the relation of *UDHR* Article 21 to youth participation in the political process. I then make a case for youth participation in environmental protection. Finally, I conclude with some reflections on the need to build linkages between governments and young people for environmental advocacy.

YOUTH AND POLITICAL PARTICIPATION

UDHR Article 21 declares people's right to political participation, i.e. the right of everyone to take part in the government of their country, directly or through representatives. Furthermore, the right to political participation can encompass diverse forms of participation, such as voting, political parties, activism, lobbying, and others. However, political participation is not only a simple form of political behaviour: it is also considered a form of political action that influences public policy in the legislative arena, local governments and other decision-making positions.

My concern is that, not every group in society – such as women, indigenous, rural populations, and the youth – have traditionally tended to participate actively or be formally represented in governmental spheres or the public service. Young people are considerably less likely to be members of, or be active within, major electoral parties. They are also less likely to engage in any form of conventional political action, compared to older age groups. Young people's under-representation in political and administrative elites is especially surprising.[35]

It is tempting to argue that youth political participation and representation depend on many factors, such as political culture, political systems, even socio-economic changes and the way democracy is (or is not) exercised. In that respect, states should adopt progressive measures to ensure democratic and adequate representation of (minority) groups in government, and actively involve them in the formulation of laws and policies that affect them.[35] Political participation and representation are fundamental rights to which the youth are entitled. These rights encourage young people to take control over matters and decisions directly affecting them in the spheres of education, employment, and the environment, among others.

POLITICAL PARTICIPATION AND ENVIRONMENT

The environment is currently one of the most important (and controversial) subjects under discussion in the political realm. Climate change, carbon dioxide emissions, toxic pollution, clean water and environmental sustainability are only just a few issues that people, as active citizens, must know about and should understand in terms of how changes will affect (and indeed already are affecting) life on the planet. As suggested by Alexander Kiss, "[. . .] the state of the environment has an impact on the implementation of human rights, as for example the right to life, health, food and housing" (1992:36). Without the right to environmental safety, any other human rights cannot be fully enjoyed.

Moreover, it is important to understand that citizens' participation and environmental protection are not issues isolated from one another. On the contrary, a very important relation is found in both the literature and in international legislation. For instance, Principle 10 of the *Rio Declaration on Environment and Development*,[37] i.e. the principle of access to information and participation in decisions, states that:

> Environmental issues are best handled with the participation of all concerned citizens, at the relevant level. At the national level, each individual shall have appropriate access to information concerning the environment that is held by public authorities, including information on hazardous materials and activities in their communities, and the opportunity to participate in decision-making processes. States shall facilitate and encourage public awareness and participation by making information widely available. Effective access to judicial and administrative proceedings, including redress and remedy, shall be provided.[38]

Citizen participation should be regarded as a major tool for environmental protection. States should then guarantee that individuals enjoy the right to participation in decision-making processes, and that they have access to information and to justice in environmental matters in order to advocate for a healthy environment that will allow the enjoyment of all human rights. In this sense, the *Aarhus Convention*[39] is viewed as an important contribution to the involvement of the citizenship in environmental protection. As pointed out by ex-UN Secretary-General Kofi Annan:

> Although regional in scope, the significance of the Aarhus Convention is global. It is by far the most impressive elaboration of principle 10 of the Rio Declaration, which stresses the need for citizens' participation in environmental issues and for access to information on the environment held by public authorities. As such it is the most ambitious venture in the area of "environmental democracy" so far undertaken under the auspices of the United Nations.

The *Aarhus Convention* is a new kind of environmental agreement that links environmental rights with human rights. It acknowledges that we humans as a race owe an obligation to future generations. The convention establishes that sustainable development can be achieved only through the engagement of all stakeholders. It links governmental accountability with environmental protection. It focuses on interactions between the public and public authorities in democratic contexts. The convention thus forges a new process for public participation in the negotiation and implementation of international agreements.[40]

I believe political participation of young people is essential for implementing new ideas to heal "our world of wounds" (Aldo Leopold, as cited in Hunter, David, James Salzman and Durwood Zaelke, (1998) *International Environmental Law and Policy,* Foundation Press). The world will experience some of the most dramatic changes in human history and I am convinced that youth in every country who assume decision-making positions can (and should) contribute to finding sustainable solutions to change policies that come across as inefficient.

FOCUS ON LATIN AMERICA

In Latin America, for example, according to a survey conducted in 2004 by the *Latinobarómetro Corporation,* the percentage of youth participation in conventional political action and decision-making processes is very low (considering that youth represent more than 18 per cent of the total population).[41] Only 12 per cent claimed to have contact with official authorities, while merely 7 per cent reported working for a political party. Most young people between 18-24 years of age have participated in 'non conventional' political activities, such as signing a petition (15 per cent) and working for other groups, such as street protests or activist groups.[42]

Additionally, the *United Nations World Youth Report 2007* (*UNWYR*) states that young people in Latin America are often unable to participate in political process because they have limited resources and simply have to struggle to survive. A substantial number of youth migrate to other countries, seeking to escape enduring socio-economic pressures at home. Therefore, forced to concentrate on basic survival, there is a growing number of youth who are forced to withdraw from the political process.[42]

In light of these conditions, youth participation in political decision-making poses a real challenge to both governments and the youth itself. Each country and the United Nations should support the promotion and creation of mechanisms that involve youth representation in governments.[44] This would represent the strengthening of democracy to build effective governance for the protection of Human Rights. The challenge remains, however, to find the most effective way to promote and include youth representatives in governments. Some experts have pointed to civic education and training. I believe education in that matter should be one of the key priorities on upcoming political agenda.

'GREEN' YOUTH ENGAGEMENT

According to the *United Nations Environment Programme* (*UNEP*), over 70 per cent of the Earth's land surface might be affected by the impact of roads, mining, cities and other infrastructure developments over the next thirty years unless urgent action is taken.[45] In Uganda, for instance, 80 per cent of youth aged between 15 and 24 do not have access to safe drinking water (*UN World Youth Report 2007*). On the whole, there is an urgent need to find new ways to protect the planet, an imperative need to improve environmental policies, to find real solutions to avoid the adversities of negative actions that damage human well-being and perpetuate environmental damage. I believe that each one of us has the political duty to contribute towards a better world. Youth, as change agents, should participate in environmental politics. Enthusiastic, creative and innovative, they can invoke more changes in environmental strategies in their capacity of Environmental Young Leaders.

GOVERNMENT AND YOUTH: GETTING INVOLVED

In my own experience as a leadership trainer, young people's involvement in public life can change the way politics are played out. Engaging young people with an understanding of Human Rights in decision-making processes can create new politics for effective governance and the strengthening of democracy. Youth participation involves an intriguing combination of continuity with the past mixed with a variety of new perspectives, values and energy.[46]

Encouraging young people to participate in central and local governments as well as political parties can produce positive results because young people bring with them new ideas and alternative ways of making policy that, in my view, will have a stronger and better impact on society and development than the same-old strategies. For instance, young participants in the Friedrich Ebert Foundation (*FES*) *Agentes de Cambio* (i.e. *Agents of Change*) leadership programme come from a variety of social backgrounds and represent different political positions. They are trained to deal respectfully, tolerantly, and responsibly with people with different views within the group, and to practise processes of political decision-making. This programme aims to strengthen social democracy in Central America by enabling young professionals working in the media, trade unions, political parties, cooperative societies and other social organisations to develop political knowledge, social competence, and concepts related values. This programme is run by the FES offices in Guatemala, Honduras, El Salvador, Nicaragua, Costa Rica, and Panama, which work as a Central American Network of young leaders.

During this capacity-building programme, participants hone their democratic leadership skills, apply innovative concepts in fieldwork for the political advocacy and empower themselves through knowledge creation, social abilities, and positive attitudes. The young participants also strengthen their accountability, responsibility and commitment to improve their communities, countries and regions. After this experience, young people find themselves strongly motivated to occupy decision-making and public positions, while promoting a political leadership free of corruption and focused on concrete results.

Education and training also offer benefits for governments. By empowering young people to participate more in fully public service and decision-making processes, young people become engaged as partners in shaping better societies (*UNWYR 2007*). Consider, for example, linkages between governments and the youth in order to bring about justice and positive change in human rights and environmental issues. Well-trained young leaders can certainly assume responsibility to influence public policy in the social, economic, political, and cultural spheres and to protect the public from environmental hazards by stepping back to actually protect the natural world.

POLITICAL DUTY

A major conclusion from this essay is that the content of any one human right is also the content of its corresponding duty.[47] The human right to political participation is the duty to participate in the political life of a country. The right to a clean and healthy environment is the duty to be responsible towards that environment. Young people's political participation is a primary duty to contribute towards the prevention of environmental harm.

As pointed out by Thomas Meyer and Nicole Breyer (2007:53), "participation in decision-making ensures the legitimisation and realisation of basic rights in all areas of social cooperation". So, political participation impels citizens' interests to be realised and represented democratically in social decision-making processes. I believe that youth engagement in decision-making processes can create new progressive politics focused on the fulfilment of Human Rights and Social Justice.

REFERENCES

Agenda 21, Chapter 25: Children and Youth in Sustainable Development, UN website available at: http://www.un.org/esa/sustdev/documents/agenda21/english/agenda21chapter25.htm

Fahmy Eldin, 2006, *Young Citizens: Young People's Involvement in Politics and Decision*, Ashgate Publishing Ltd, Surrey, United Kingdom

Griffin, James, 2008, *On Human Rights*, Oxford University Press, New York

Hunter, David, James Salzman and Durwood Zaelke, 1998, *International Environmental Law and Policy*, Foundation Press, US

Kiss A, 1991, 'Concept and Possible Implications of the Right to Environment', in Mahoney, K E and Mahoney P, (Ed) 1993, *Human*

Rights in the Twenty-First Century, Kluwer Academic Publishers, The Netherlands

Latinobarometro 2004: www.latinobarometro.org

Meyer Thomas, and Breyer Nicole, 2007, *The Future of Social Democracy*, Friedrich Ebert Stiftung Politische Acdemie, published by M Sengupta for Samskriti, New Delhi, India

Pierre Claude, Richard and Weston, Burns H, (Ed), 2006, *Human Rights in the World Community: Issues and Action*, University of Pennsylvania Press, Philadelphia

Right to Environment initiative, website, http://www.righttoenvironment.org

Rio Declaration on Environment and Development, United Nations Environment Programme website available at http://www.unep.org/Documents.Multilingual/Default.asp?DocumentID=78&ArticleID=1163

The Aarhus Convention: An Implementation Guide, 2000, United Nations Economic Commission for Europe (UNECE), United Nations Publication, New York and Geneva

United Nations Environment Programme (*UNEP*) website available at: http://www.unep.org

United Nations World Youth Report 2007, Department of Economic and Social Affairs, UN website: http://www.un.org/esa/socdev/unyin/wyr07.htm.

Universal Declaration of Human Rights (*UDHR*), United Nations website available at: http://www.un.org/events/humanrights/udhr60/declaration.shtml

Zukin, Cliff, Keeter Scott, Andolina Molly, Jenkins Krista, 2006, *A New Engagement?: Political Participation, Civic Life, and the Changing*, Oxford University Press, New York

Human Rights and the Environment:

Ensuring Water Quality and Environmental Sustainability

Vannaphone Manibod

It can be argued that the world is our body, and its waterways our veins that transport the Earth's nutrients to different parts of that body in order for it to live and grow. Water carries life – not only to human beings, but also to all creatures on this planet. The issue of water purity and security requires the efforts of all countries in the world. All states are responsible for maintaining water quality and ensuring environmental sustainability. In today's world, however, there are a number of water-related problems that need some serious addressing.

One such problem is the widespread lack of environmental knowledge and education among world populations. Many countries, especially developing countries, are victims to a certain degree of illiteracy due to restricted accessibility to information and education about environment protection. In my own experience, spending time with local people in villages, I have realised that many people in rural areas are generally unaware of the negative impact of their activities for the environment. For instance, people cut down trees from the mountains in large amounts without recognising that that they may create serious problems, including landslides and soil erosion. Similar activities, such as slash and burn, can also cause great damage to the atmosphere due to the release of large quantities of carbon dioxide and nitrous oxide into the air. This has been documented as one of the causes of global warming.

The natural environment is the unequivocal basis of human survival, especially for many developing countries. In poor countries, people are reliant on natural resources for their daily survival. Forests and rivers are the largest natural resource, supplying food, medicine and shelter for local populations. For instance, Lao PDR is endowed with diverse, productive and ecologically unique forests, estimated at 47 per cent of the total land area. Eighty per cent of the population lives in rural areas and are highly dependent on the local environment for subsistence farming livelihoods. However, a large majority of rural households do not have access to clean water and sanitation facilities. Therefore, when it comes to environmental problem-solving, it is not so easy to find a solution due to the lack of knowledge and education on issues of the Earth. Providing information for people through written documents is not suitable because of the low levels of literacy in the population.

Another important issue is the rapid increase in population worldwide. This has a direct impact on environmental sustainability and water quality. According to the United Nations, about one billion people around the globe still lack access to safe drinking water, while 2.5 billion lack access to basic sanitation. On a more positive note, 1.6 billion people gained access to safe water and sanitation during the 1990s. As the increase in world population clearly shows, there will be more people consuming the available natural resources, including the planet's water. When many people consume large amounts of water, the level of water in rivers is prone to a continuous drop. Water problems are easily found in poor countries, or in heavily industrialised countries producing hydropower energy.

Generating energy from hydropower requires a massive amount of water. When water is held in large qualities, a shortage of water and poor quality of water for the people to consume will ensue. People who live downstream can be affected by polluted water. Moreover, if countries upstream build dams and use huge amount of water to generate hydropower, the neighbouring countries downstream can definitely feel a negative impact. The major blow would be the lack of clean water and sanitation, which is the world's single largest cause of illness.

A final factor that might be the cause for poor water quality is the development of changes in a country. In case of industrial development, for instance, the environment is likely to be affected. For a country to develop industries, infrastructure/building is required. Whenever factories are built, toxins are produced that can pollute water, turning it into a channel of waste release. Chemicals can be harmful to the animals that live in the water, and to people who consume it. Therefore, local governments and water authorities need to consider the issue and offer concrete solutions to prevent hydro pollution. Furthermore, engaging young people in the political processes and decision-making is crucial in investing in the prevention of future environmental problems.

In conclusion, as a way to ensure environmental sustainability and quality drinking water, people around the world need to become aware of this problem and be willing to face the emerging challenges. One step at a time, we can work for everybody's maintenance and access to clean water as well as the right to the natural resources and health. We all should do our best to improve all aspects of environmental hygiene as established in Article 12 (2.b) of the *International Covenant on Economic, Social and Culture Rights* in order to make our world a better place to live in.

REFERENCES

http://www.un.org/issues/m-envir.html

http://www.un.org/millenniumgoals

National Agriculture and Forestry Research Institution, 2008, p.10, website available at: www.nafri.org.la

National Statistic of Lao PDR, 2007, Population Rate, p.30

The World Bank in Laos, Issue no 8, 2008, website available at: www.worldbank.org/lao

The Universal Declaration of Human Rights, 1984, website available at: www.un.org/overview/right.htmi, www.righttoenvironment.org

Food Security & Health

A Kenyan Perspective on Hunger, Malnutrition and Human Rights

Towards a Healthy Planet

Dickens Osano Molo

The importance of the *Millennium Development Goals* (*MDGs*) cannot be overemphasised, yet Goal 1 – *to eradicate extreme poverty and hunger* – is perhaps most pertinent to countries in Africa and Asia, where the vast majority of the world's poor live. The current global food crisis has captured the attention of the international community, given that food riots are now a common occurrence in countries like Haiti, Egypt and Somalia.[48] In my home country of Kenya, hunger and malnutrition are widespread, especially in drought-stricken dry-land areas. They constitute a real crisis (Nyariki *et al*, 2002) with several challenges continuing to hamper food security in Africa. Among these are environmental factors (such as land degradation and recurrent droughts), technological factors (like poor farming technologies and lack of farm inputs for small scale farmers), human factors (such as over-reliance on cash crops like coffee, tea and sugar cane, at the expense of food crops such as maize and beans), and socio-political factors (such as health challenges in the form of HIV/AIDS, corruption and political marginalisation, and neglect of indigenous traditional foods).

The food crisis is of great concern to the international community because it often leads to the loss of lives, starvation, malnutrition (especially among children), social unrest, and because it decreases human productivity by hampering participation in economic activities and civic engagement. I spend a lot of time doing community mobilisation work in rural western Kenya, and thus have the opportunity to talk to young people, women and men on what really are the reasons for which poverty and hunger have become so endemic in our society. I often see myself as a voice for these people, many of whom do not have a forum to express their opinions or to be heard by the country's political leadership. Deeply etched in my mind is the voice of an old woman I once talked to in one of my community interviews. She was perhaps in her late 70s and marvellously reminisced about the hopes that came with independence in 1963, when the founding President had promised three things: *to eradicate poverty, ignorance and diseases*. Today, these three problems have become worse than ever before, as millions of Kenyans face severe hunger and starvation.[49]

Agriculture is considered to be the backbone of most African economies. In Kenya, nearly 75 per cent of agricultural production is harvested by small-scale farmers, many of whom are directly dependent on grains (maize, wheat), and cash crops (mainly tea, sugarcane, rice and tobacco). However, since the early 1990s (when African governments were forced to embrace economic liberalisation), the agricultural sector has suffered severely. For example, the importation of sugar produced cheaply in foreign countries has dealt a big blow to sugar factories in western Kenya, which are unable to sell their produce in local markets and therefore unable to make payments to local farmers, who, in turn, lack income for meeting their basic needs. Furthermore, the drop in world prices of major cash crops (such as coffee and tea) has affected the local farmers' incomes, too. As a result, the majority of farmers in rural Kenya have become even poorer. With no government subsidies, many farmers cannot afford to buy farm inputs (such as fertilisers, herbicides and farm implements and machinery), which leads to low agricultural yields.[50]

The situation of starvation in Africa is further complicated by the nature of rural economy, which is highly dependent on local natural resources. For instance, in East Africa around the Lake Victoria basin (mainly western Kenya, eastern Uganda, and northern Tanzania), rural communities are highly reliant on fisheries from the lake as a source of protein. However, the decline in local fish varieties and the rising prices of the dominant fish in Lake Victoria, the Nile Perch, due to increased demand in Europe has effectively meant that the locals, with low income, cannot afford to buy Nile Perch. Not surprisingly, the highest levels of malnutrition and poverty in East Africa are found in the Lake Victoria region (Awange & Ong'ang'a, 2006).

Moreover, the impact of HIV/AIDS on food security is also acute, especially in the rural areas. Indeed, without effective policies and strategies to reduce the incidence of HIV/AIDS among young people, who form the bulk of the farm labour sector, it will not be easy to ensure food production that may meet the growing demands of a rising human population. Most families affected by HIV/AIDS spend a fortune to pay for the medical costs incurred in treatment, and this effectively eats away at the meagre earnings they have, as well as any savings in form of assets they may possess (such as livestock, land and other productive assets).

THE HUMAN RIGHTS FRAMEWORK

There is growing recognition in political and developmental circles of the necessity to embrace basic needs (food, shelter, clothes) as human rights, and intellectual discourse on this matter has become common since the 1980s (Streeten 1980; Weigel 1986; Miller, 2007). The 'basic needs-as-human rights' framework recognises, for instance, that hunger, poverty, lack of education, and other essential social services entail a denial of human rights and can be tackled as human rights issues. Furthermore, international and regional human rights instruments acknowledge the right to a dignified life for all human beings irrespective of race, gender and cultural affiliations. Article 25 (1) of the *Universal Declaration of Human Rights* (*UDHR*) partly states that "Everyone has the right to a standard of living adequate for the health and well-being of himself and of his family, including food, clothing, housing and medical care and necessary social services . . .".[51] Considering this emphatic statement, there is actually no reason for the world to allow more than 800 million people to suffer from hunger and food insecurity, when the productive capacity does exist to provide them with more the necessary amounts of food.

Indeed, civil society groups such as the UK charity *Action Aid* have recently begun to frame advocacy for basic needs in terms of human rights: "Everyone has the right to be free from hunger, and this right is perhaps the most fundamental of all. Without food, no one can have life or health", states *Action Aid*.[52] In 1981, the African political leadership adopted the 'African [Banjul] Charter on Human and Peoples' Rights', expressing political recognition of human rights for all in Africa.[53] This charter forms a basis for human rights advocacy in African countries. Attention must also be paid to minorities and marginalised groups in Africa.

For example, food security and hunger tend to affect women and children more severely than other populations. In this regard, Article 15 of the 'Protocol to the *African Charter on Human and Peoples' Rights on the Rights of Women in Africa*' recognises the 'Right to Food Security'; it calls for the provision of women with access to clean drinking water, sources of domestic fuel, land, and the means of producing nutritious food, as well as for the establishment of adequate systems of supply and storage to ensure food security.[54] It can be argued that the challenge now is not a lack of a human rights framework to the right to food: the new challenge that remains is to breathe life into these existing frameworks, particularly the *UDHR*, and the *African Charter on Human and People's Rights* to serve as instruments for the eradication of hunger in Africa and the world over.

Although this essay focuses on Africa, the food crisis, hunger and malnutrition are common in other developing regions of the world, as well. For example, in Haiti, one of the countries afflicted by food riots in 2008, three quarters of the population earn less than a dollar a day, and one in five children is chronically malnourished.[55] Because hunger is pervasive and hard to measure, the levels of malnutrition in a population may offer a clearer picture. The *World Bank* observes that many countries in East Asia, Latin America, and Eastern Europe are heavily affected by malnutrition (*World Bank 2006*). The most striking aspect of hunger has been evidenced by the global food crisis, as heightened by rising food commodity prices.[56]

The crisis has now reached such proportions that even in Thailand, which produces 10 million more tons of rice than it consumes and is the world's largest rice exporter, supermarkets have placed signs limiting the amount of rice shoppers are allowed to purchase.[57] Other countries outside Africa that have been affected by the food crisis include Indonesia, Malaysia, and Mexico, to mention but a few. The food crisis is exacerbated by the competition between bio-fuels and food, and increase in climate change and weather-related events which destroy crops and reduce food supplies. For example, among the Pacific Island countries, ocean warming, frequent tropical cyclones, flash floods and droughts are likely to have a devastating impact on food production systems (*FAO*, 2008). Global and local solutions are, therefore, imperative.

LOOKING FORWARD AS A YOUTH

Young people today are growing up in a world that is faced with myriad challenges with respect to political governance, human rights, environmental destruction, and lack of democracy. At the same time, it is a world of unimaginable opportunities ranging from technological progress to growth in financial capital and wealth. Unfortunately, the massive wealth in the world remains in the hands of a few, and the divide between the rich and the poor continues to rise. It is therefore incumbent upon young people to work for the eradication of poverty and hunger, and to uphold the rights of every world citizen to basic needs, i.e. the rights to food, shelter, clothing and education. Given the current food crisis, and the global financial turmoil, it is easy to become pessimistic, yet young people must be torch-bearers of hope. There are many avenues for doing so, and there are worthy models to emulate. In

Kenya, Diana Onyonyi, a 14-year-old girl, has been a regular participant in the annual *Freedom from Hunger Walk* since the age of three and has raised an estimated 1 million Ksh (US$ 20,000), a feat which won her a commendation from Kenya's President in 2006.[58]

Challenging hunger cannot effectively be achieved in the absence of a compact between the global north and the south which is to include collaboration, advocacy and awareness-raising about hunger among people in the north. Young Beau Dexter of *North Scott High School*, Iowa, USA, profoundly articulated the food and malnutrition problems in Kenya for a larger audience at the *2005 World Food Prize* (Beau 2005). Most importantly, young people must be involved in shaping food policies. In Kenya, youths under the banner of *ActionAid* through *Activista*, a network of students and young people across rich and poor countries campaigning for a hunger and poverty-free world, have recently demanded their inclusion in the government policy formulation process.[59] The foregoing examples show that young people can and do play an important role in fashioning solutions to hunger and malnutrition.

THE WAY FORWARD

The problem of hunger and malnutrition is both structural and conditional. In the former case, it is recognised that there is enough food in the world to feed everyone, yet its distribution is the problem (especially given the wasteful consumption in industrialised countries). In the latter, geography and environmental factors limit the production of food in some places, such as the Horn of Africa, thus leading to famine and perennial reliance on food aid in some areas.[60] Solutions must, therefore, be multifaceted. They must involve increased food production, as the latter also ensures fair distribution of food among world populations. Below I discuss three options, but recognise that there are many other options that may be considered.

First, despite the traditionally unexploited role of indigenous foods (such as local varieties of vegetables, roots and tubers) in enhancing the nutritional status of the people, governmental policy for agriculture in Africa has ignored this important and cheap food for the rural poor. In fact, indigenous knowledge on traditional farming and breeding techniques as practised by our grandfathers' generation is now being lost due to lack of proper documentation. The loss of indigenous technological practices is further exacerbated by losses in biological varieties of wild crops that harbour the potential to produce new varieties of food in the future. I would, therefore, see the need for various groups, governments, NGOs, civil society and scientists to link campaigns for eradicating hunger and malnutrition to the preservation of ecological biodiversity and traditional indigenous knowledge.

Second, in Africa, intensive farming techniques that involve use of chemicals and fertilisers may be difficult for the poor to adopt because the latter usually lack the capital for purchasing farm inputs without subsidies from the government. At the same time, said techniques can lead to higher crop yields, if support can be accorded to the farmers. There is already a debate regarding the potential and pitfalls for genetically modified crops.[61] In any case, the lack of capital opens up the opportunity for small-scale farmers to adopt environment-friendly farming methods. For instance, I have advocated for sustainable agriculture that is based on agro-forestry techniques, such as use of manure, proper tillage, nursery gardening, row-cropping, as well as nature-based income activities like bee-keeping for honey production, and poultry farming among youth groups in Kenya.

Third, another instrumental factor in ending hunger pertains to the political leadership and governance at the local, national and global levels. In Kenya as in most other African countries, the inequitable distribution of resources has an impact on conditional factors such as transport, communication, education and health services, all of which are key determinants of poverty and food security. Africa, as a continent, has witnessed pathetic leadership devoid of respect to human rights, with most leaders being driven by corruption and ethnic chauvinism. Who could have imagined that Zimbabwe, once considered a bread basket of Africa, would be in such a food-deficit as to depend on food aid from the west at the turn of the century? What would Africa be like if perennial dictators such a Mobutu Seseko of Zaire (now DRC Congo) had not swindled money from state coffers to keep in unmarked personal bank accounts in Switzerland? These questions require that, as young people, we promote and advocate for responsible leadership in our communities by holding leaders accountable, and by exposing corruption.

FINAL WORDS

There is no doubt that the human rights framework is sufficient to ensure the eradication of hunger and malnutrition worldwide. It is ironical indeed that the convergence of the worst global food and financial crises in recent times should take place during the commemoration of the 60th anniversary of the *Universal Declaration of Human Rights*. This then is the most opportune time for humanity to reflect deeply on the conception of human rights as articulated in both theory and practice. The human rights concept should be expanded to guarantee *human security*, i.e. security from fear, from hunger, and from all forms of threats to humanity.

Author's acknowledgments to P Osano and S Mobilia, for insights and informed discussions.

REFERENCES

Awange J, and O Ong'ang'a, 2006, *Lake Victoria: Ecology, Resources and Environment*, Springer Verlag

Dexter B, 2005, *Food Production in Kenya and its Relationship to Malnutrition*, Essay (World Food Prize)

http://www.worldfoodprize.org/assets/YouthInstitute/05proceedings/NorthcottHighSchool.pdf

FAO, 2008, *Climate Change and Food Security in Pacific Island Countries*, online available at: http://www.fao.org/docrep/011/i0530e/i0530e00.htm

Miller D, 2007, *Human Rights, Basic Needs, and Scarcity*, Centre for the Study of Social Justice & Department of Politics and International Relations,

Working Paper Series, SJ007, Nyariki D M, S L Wigins, and J K Imungi, 2002, *Levels and Causes of Household Food and Nutrition Insecurity in Dryland Kenya*, Ecology of Food and Nutrition, 41: 155-176

Streeten P, 1980, *Basic Needs and Human Rights*, World Development, 8:107-111

Weigel V B, 1986, *The Basic Needs Approach: Overcoming the Poverty of Homo Economicus*, World Development, 14(12):1423-1434

World Bank, 2006, *Repositioning Nutrition as Central to Development: A Strategy for Large-Scale Action*

The Right to Food in the Light of the Millennium Development Goals and the Universal Declaration of Human Rights

Angelina Reif

Eight-hundred and fifty-two million people in today's world – i.e. more than the populations of the United States of America, Canada and the European Union put together – do not have sufficient food to eat (FAO 2003). In other words, one-sixth of the world's population suffers from hunger. Furthermore, ten million people die of hunger every year – which translates into 25,000 human beings a day. Moreover, more than 300 million children are undernourished. Even more alarmingly, every five seconds a child dies of the consequences of malnutrition and chronic hunger, in particular contracted diseases and infections (FAO 2003).

Hunger and malnutrition are the number-one risk to global health today, taking a higher death toll than AIDS, malaria and tuberculosis combined (WHO 2002:37). As Philip Alston and Katarina Tomaševski (1984:7) had noticed almost a decade earlier: "these statistics make hunger by far the most flagrant and widespread of all serious human rights abuses." Likewise, in its resolution 1998/23, the *Commission on Human Rights* reaffirmed that hunger constitutes an outrage and a violation of human dignity. Hunger is not exclusive to developing or war-torn countries. Many developed countries also face food insecurity among their poorest populations. All this is in a world which already produces more than enough food to feed the global population (Smith and van den Anker 2005:135).

Although the right to food has been endorsed more often than most other human rights, its violations have been more comprehensive and systematic than probably those of any other right. As the right to food is already firmly established as an international human right, it is high time to ensure its universal recognition and implementation.

FOOD IN INTERNATIONAL HUMAN RIGHTS LAW

The right to food emerges in the context of the broader human right to an adequate standard of living. Article 25(1) of the *Universal Declaration of Human Rights* (*UDHR*) states, "everyone has the right to a standard of living adequate for the health and well-being of himself and his family, including food". The right to food is a basic right, in the sense that it is necessary for the enjoyment of all other rights. Without food, one cannot concentrate or work effectively. And, without that capacity to work, one cannot buy food. Thus, hunger is both a cause and a consequence of poverty, as it develops a vicious circle.

The first goal of the *Millennium Development Goals* (*MDGs*) focuses on reducing both poverty and hunger. Although the importance of these issues can be recognised by the fact that they head the list of the *MDGs*, hunger is far behind track. Even more alarmingly is the fact that the overall trend is now one of regression, rather than progression towards the realisation of the right to food. In fact, hunger has been on the increase since the 1996 World Food Summit.

In the past, the discussions about hunger and the responses to it were mostly based on compassion, a consequence of which was that the 'beneficiaries' of feeding programmes were reduced to passive objects disenfranchised of the right to an enabling environment that would allow them to take care of their own livelihoods through personal efforts and resources. Contrary to these basic needs-oriented strategies, a human rights approach regards individuals as active subjects and 'claim holders' (FAO 1998:vii). Hence, this approach introduces a normative basis as well as an accountability dimension. Nowadays, there is increasing recognition that access to adequate food as a fundamental human right implies a legal obligation. Yet, sadly enough, justiciability[62] still remains a virtually unexplored territory (*FLAN* 2008:5).

The *Voluntary Guidelines* adopted by the FAO Council and approved by all FAO member states in November 2004 represent a human rights-based practical tool to address the shortcoming of legal instruments that guarantee the right to food by empowering the poor and hungry to claim their rights. Although the *Guidelines* do not establish legally binding obligations for international organisations or states, the latter are strongly encouraged to apply them in developing their strategies, policies programmes and activities (FAO 2004:vi-vii). Even though human rights apply to all persons regardless of their nationality, the obligations are primarily domestic. International force would only be obtained if the international community were obliged to take appropriate action when national governments fail to ensure the realisation of those rights. To this day, there is neither a procedure nor a firm commitment to provide the right to food with an enforcement mechanism. The need for such a system is evident, since, even if national governments carry the primary legal responsibility for the realisation of human rights, these burdens morally fall on each one of us to some greater or lesser extent.

However, there is still little recognition of the idea that the international community as a whole holds such obligations. Human rights obligations are treated as if they end at national borders. This is evidenced by the fact that international governmental organisations represent and collectively act on behalf of the states.

UNITED NATIONS BODIES

The severity of the problem of unequal access to food can be observed by the fact that the *World Food Programme* (*WFP*) embodies the largest humanitarian agency in the world. But not only is the

WFP concerned with food and nutrition, but there are also other prominent international organisations active in the field such as the *Food and Agriculture Organisation* (*FAO*) of the United Nations, the *International Fund for Agricultural Development* (*IFAD*), the *World Health Organisation* (*WHO*) and the *United Nations' International Children's Emergency Fund* (*UNICEF*). Yet, hunger and malnutrition are only a part of their broad agenda. I argue that the *FAO*, the *WFP* and the *IFAD* in particular should become more institutionally sensitive to the fact that

> aspects of the right to food are their main purpose, and more willing to take a rights approach as well as taking part in the effort of the United Nations to integrate human rights in general into all aspects of its work (Mary Robinson, in: FAO 1998:vii).

The efforts of the various organisations and programmes would be much more effective if a common understanding and a shared direction for eliminating hunger and malnutrition were accomplished amongst human rights institutions and the development agencies, as well as if the separate pieces of the individual organisations were coordinated as part of a large, long-term, goal-directed programme. The coordinating function is already carried partly out by the *United Nations System Standing Committee on Nutrition* (*SCN*). Furthermore, the activities of the intergovernmental organisations should be consolidated in a cogent programme of action, which should initially focus on the questions of which locales could benefit the most from its intervention. For calling forth resource commitments and designing the institutional arrangements required, a modest and limited goal should be pursued, for instance, that of securing that no child under three years of age goes hungry. The new programme of action should also consider the creation of a new global body (comparable to that of the United Nations Human Rights Treaty Bodies) with monitoring and coordinating functions that would ensure that the terms of the plan and the agreements made by the agencies are effectively carried out. Local and international civil society organisations should be part of the new system.

Two major shortcomings are inherent in the initiatives at the global level. Firstly, their focus is on national and not on global plans of action. Secondly, the intergovernmental organisations are viewed as mere facilitators, rather than as major actors. The only way to reduce chronic food insecurity is to coordinate food and nutrition activities among intergovernmental organisations and to press and help national governments addressing the problem of inadequate food among their own people, using resources of their own. As suggested by George Kent (2005:229), the *WFP* should make it known that, in providing food supplies for development, it would favour those nations that are working to establish clear and effective entitlements for the most needy in their nations.

GLOBAL ACTION REQUIRED

The capacity of the world to produce food is given (Smith and van den Anker 2005:135). The absence of resources is rather a lack of political will than a structural incapacity. Our planet produces more than enough food for every man, woman, and child to live healthy and productive lives. Just one week of subsidies given to farmers in the developed world would cover the annual cost of food aid (*Bread for the World Institute* 2003:2). The *United Nations Development Programme* (*UNDP*) estimates that the basic health and nutrition needs of the world's poorest people could be met for an additional $13 billion a year. Animal lovers in the United States and Europe spend more than that amount on pet food each year (*Bread for the World* website).

The full attention and resources of the international community need to be devoted to addressing the concerns of nations and people affected by food insecurity. In doing so, it should be borne in mind that the right to food is not about charity, but about ensuring that all people have the capacity to feed themselves in dignity. The core task is not to feed people, but to create enabling conditions so that every human being has a decent opportunity to provide for oneself and one's family. Planning the ending of hunger and malnutrition has to begin with the reconfiguration of social and economic forces and institutions so that they no longer contribute to the production of poverty and hunger. As Kent (2005:225-226) has pointed out, these challenges are largely political, having to do with ownership and control of land and other factors of production, and they are largely economic, having to do with the allocation of resources and the determination of prices.

INDIVIDUAL CONTRIBUTION

Not everything is about politics and economy. An integral part of social change is the shaping of public opinion. As one single person may feel powerless, pointing out some possibilities to act would empower individuals to join the fight against hunger. The abandonment of subsistence farming, the widespread disregard for domestic needs and the displacement of local farmers are some of the problems caused by large landowners, trans-/multinational companies and agribusinesses. These actors can be only induced to refrain from acts that threaten or even violate people's human rights by publicly exposing them in newspapers or reports presented to the United Nations. Likewise, their mention in protest letters drafted by outraged people from all over the world helps put these actors in check. In addition to 'naming and shaming' the multinationals, discerning consumers should boycott the products of those that exploit local farmers and undercut the prices for commodities.

The need to support local farmers is beyond question. How to bolster small producers in order to compensate for the imbalances of power in the food production and distribution chain still remains a matter of considerable debate. In order to avoid repeating old mistakes, technocratic solutions, driven from above, should be replaced by a bottom-up approach that promotes the emergence of local solutions, which are much more reliant on the active participation and needs of smallhold producers. One possible attempt to counteract the dependency of developing countries on food imports, monocultures[63] and 'cash crop'[64] production might be the implementation of sustainable farming programmes, which have been proven to alleviate poverty while keeping people connected to their land and their traditional farming lifestyles.

Moreover, this type of programmes offers the opportunity to engage university students and university resources in a collaborative, reciprocal, holistic and interdisciplinary approach to hunger and poverty alleviation. According to the *Voluntary Guidelines* mentioned above, national states should strengthen

> developing country university and technical faculties of agriculture-related disciplines [. . .] to carry out both education and research functions, and engaging universities throughout the world in training developing country agriculturalists, scientists and businessmen (FAO 2004:xx).

Based on mutual exchange, the collaboration on the one hand imparts indigenous knowledge of traditional farming and breeding techniques while on the other hand, it provides local farmers with technical assistance and natural resources (such as soil management, modern irrigation techniques, food storage, and conservation methods) in order to reduce post-harvest losses, access to seeds and fertilisers, pest-management practices, as well as research on new adaptable crop varieties. This approach is purpose-and goal-oriented in so far as there is a

> lack of support given to the agricultural sector by African governments (Final Declaration of the African Network for Promotion of the Right to Food, in Brot für die Welt, ICCO and FIAN 2008:16),

despite the fact that agriculture is not only the backbone of the economies of most African countries but also the main source of revenue for food for the African people.

The average daily expenditure on food in the developed world is ten dollars. *WFP* food rations cost 29 cents per day (*WFP* 2003a). For 19 cents, one can feed a hungry child in school for a day (*WFP* 2003b). Research shows that free school lunches not only boost performance, but also may bring about an increase in attendance rates by 100 per cent (*WFP* website). Not only will children be our future leaders, but even now they exert a strong influence on their social surroundings. They are part and parcel of civil society and thus their sensitive and targeted education is essential for the future of critical public opinion. Only politically mature citizens will have the ability to make the world a better place.

FINAL WORDS

The nature of the food crisis transcends national boundaries, and problems faced in one part of the world have ripple effects on other parts as well. In "an age of problems without passports" (Kofi Annan, on the *UNIS Vienna* website), tackling the issue of hunger requires collective responsibilities and concerted measures from governments and international agencies in order

> to rectify those inequalities that have contributed to trigger the emergency and that now threaten to perpetuate it (Louise Arbour, in: *Brot für die Welt, ICCO* and *FIAN* 2008:35).

Only if the international community holds respect for the dignity of every human being, regardless of his or her status, will there be hope for the abolition of the

> intolerable inequalities that affect millions through no fault of their own (Louise Arbour, in: *Brot für die Welt, ICCO* and *FIAN* 2008: 36).

Freedom from hunger is the only right which has been called 'fundamental' in international human rights law (Smith and van den Anker, 2005:324). As hunger is one of the most widespread threats to life, it should be treated at the same level as the right to life. But, although all human rights are said to be interdependent (i.e. they should be treated holistically in order to ensure human survival and development), socio-economic rights are still not given the same priority as civil and political rights. But only integrated, justiciable human rights guarantees can provide the poor and marginalised with opportunities to assert their needs and interests in developmental processes.

The governments may be politically committed to the right to food but for which there are not yet legal remedies. As long as this right is placed within the political realm of rhetoric rather than within the normative domain of priority setting and allocation of resources the commitment in resolution 55/2 of the Millennium Summit "to freeing the entire human race from want" will remain an empty gesture. If the right to food is to play a meaningful role, measures enabling the realisation of this right as well as a number of institutional factors must be addressed and put in place. Justiciability of human rights is necessary to ensure the material conditions for a life in dignity. The right to food is part of a larger challenge of human solidarity and freedom. Up to now we are far from the practical realisation of this goal.

REFERENCES

Alston, Philip and Toma evski, Katarina (Ed), 1984, *The Right to Food*, Dordrecht: Martinus Nijhoff

Bread for the World Institute, 2003, *Agriculture in the Global Economy*

Bread for the World website: http://www.bread.org (accessed 29 June 2008)

Brot für die Welt, ICCO (Interchurch Organisation for Development Cooperation) and FIAN (FoodFirst Informations-und Aktions-Netzwerk), 2008, *Right to Food and Nutrition Watch, The World Food Crisis and the Right to Food*, Hochheim am Main

FAO (Food and Agriculture Organisation), 2004, *Report of the Intergovernmental Working Group for the Elaboration of a Set of Voluntary Guidelines to Support the Progressive Realisation of the Right to Adequate Food in the Context of National Food Security*, IGWG RTFG 5/REP 1. Rome

FAO (Food and Agriculture Organisation), 2003, *State of Food Insecurity in the World*

FAO (Food and Agriculture Organisation), 1998, *The Right to Food in Theory and Practice*, Rome

FIAN (FoodFirst Informations-und Aktions-Netzwerk), 2008, *How to Promote the Justiciability of the Human Right to Food*, Heidelberg

Kent George, 2005, *Freedom from Want: The Human Right to Adequate Food*, Georgetown University Press, Washington DC

Smith, Rhona K M and Anker, Christien van den (Ed), 2005, *The Essentials of . . . Human Rights*, Hodder Arnold, London

UNIS (United Nations Information Service) Vienna website, http://www.unis.unvienna.org/unis/pressrels/2003/sgsm8922.html, *Multilateralism Crucial in 'Age of Problems without Passports', Secretary-General Tells African-American Civil Society Leaders*, Press Release SG/SM/8922 of 8 October 2003 (accessed 26 December 2008)

WFP (World Food Programme) website, http://www.wfp.org, *Facts and Figures on Child Hunger, Investing in Children's Education* (accessed 28 June 2009)

WFP (World Food Programme), 2003a, *Hunger Facts*

WFP (World Food Programme), 2003b, *School Feeding Global Report*

WHO (World Health Organisation), 2002, *The World Health Report 2002, Reducing Risks, Promoting Healthy Life*, Geneva

The World Bank in Laos, Issue no 8, 2008, website available at: www.worldbank.org/lao

The Universal Declaration of Human Rights, 1984, website available at: www.un.org/overview/right.htmi, www.righttoenvironment.org

The Internet as a Means of Bringing Information on HIV/AIDS to the African Population

Andrea Labruto

Since 1981, when the first cases of AIDS were identified in the United States and later in Africa, the HIV/AIDS epidemic has spread across the globe to such an extent that it has now become a pandemic.[65] The latest estimates from *UNAIDS* and the *World Health Organisation* (*WHO*) indicate that the number of people living with HIV/AIDS globally rose from 29.5 million in 2001 to 33 million in 2007. Most alarmingly, the majority of people living with HIV are unaware that they are infected.[66] More than 95 percent of people living with the disease reside in low-and middle-income countries, where most new HIV infections and AIDS-related deaths occur. Sub-Saharan Africa,[67] the hardest-hit region, is home to two-thirds (i.e. 67 per cent) of people living with HIV/AIDS, which amounts to 22.0 million people (in other words, about 11–12 per cent of the world population).[68] Furthermore, 90 per cent of the world's children affected by HIV/AIDS also live in that region.

HIV/AIDS & THE HUMAN RIGHTS FRAMEWORK

The fight against the HIV pandemic has confirmed that the promotion and protection of human rights constitute an essential component in preventing the transmission and reducing the social impact of HIV/AIDS. In particular, the linkage between human rights and effective HIV programmes is evident in the fact that the incidence of HIV is disproportionately high among certain populations considered vulnerable. Lack of human rights protection places these vulnerable populations at a higher risk of contracting HIV/AIDS. Article 26 of the *Universal Declaration of Human Rights* (*UDHR*) states that:

> Everyone has the right to education . . . Education shall be directed to the full development of the human personality and to the strengthening of respect for human rights and fundamental freedoms. It shall promote understanding, tolerance and friendship . . .

Thus, both children and adults are entitled to the right to receive HIV-related education, particularly in terms of prevention and healthcare.

Access to HIV education is a vital component of effective prevention and healthcare programmes. It is the State's obligation to ensure, in every cultural and religious tradition, that appropriate means are identified for effective HIV information to be included in educational curricula inside and outside schools. In particular, states should, through educational campaigns, promote understanding, respect, tolerance and non-discrimination of persons living with HIV.[69] In the year 2000, all United Nations member countries signed a consensus declaration with time-bound and measurable goals to pursue in order to fight global poverty, hunger, disease, illiteracy, environmental degradation and discrimination against women. This declaration became known as the *Millennium Development Goals* (*MDGs*).

MDG Goal Number 6, in particular, addresses the combat of HIV/AIDS, malaria and other diseases. It is subdivided into three targets, with Target A concerning specifically the fight of the HIV/AIDS pandemic. The international framework of 8 goals and 21 targets was complemented by 60 technical indicators to measure progress. As many as four indicators relate to Target A of Goal 6.

One of them, indicator 6.3, measures the impact of correct information on the HIV pandemic by means of the percentage of the world population aged 15-24 that: (a) can correctly identify the two major ways of preventing the sexual transmission of HIV (condoms and monogamy); (b) can reject the two most common local misconceptions about HIV transmission; and (3) know that a healthy-looking person can transmit HIV. However, since there are currently not enough surveys to allow us to calculate the indicator as defined above, *UNICEF* (in collaboration with *UNAIDS* and the *WHO*) have developed two proxy indicators that represent two components of the actual indicator: (a) the percentage of women and men aged 15-24 who know that a person can protect himself or herself from HIV infection by 'consistent use of condom'; and (b) the percentage of women and men aged 15-24 who know a healthy-looking person can transmit HIV (as summarised under the title of the official MDG indicator 6.3 as the "proportion of the/a population aged 15-24 years with comprehensive correct knowledge of HIV/AIDS").

Unfortunately, the latest report of MDG indicators (published 2007, seven years after the MDGs Declaration) states that, though slight declines in HIV prevalence among young people since 2000/2001 were reported in eight of the eleven African countries where sufficient information was available to assess trends, general prevention measures are failing to keep pace with the growth of the pandemic. For instance, in sub-Saharan Africa, less than a third of the local young men and just over a fifth of the young women demonstrated a comprehensive and correct knowledge of HIV/AIDS transmission and prevention. The disappointing failure of developing people's awareness in less developed countries warrants new strategies for the circulation of information, especially among the youngest sectors of the population.

CROSS-REFERENCES

Talk about the HIV pandemic has enhanced global consciousness of health inequality, and catalysed unprecedented action to confront some of the world's most serious developmental challenges. No disease in human history has ever prompted a comparable mobilisation of political, financial, and human resources. The movement towards universal access to HIV prevention, treatment, care and support is serving as an effective vehicle for mobilising civil society. The role of information spread in this context is of paramount importance. The case of Namibia, for example, is paradigmatic for its efforts to provide better and better information to its population. In recent years, the Namibian government has taken steps to strengthen the country's response to HIV/AIDS. Over the last two years, the country more than doubled its domestic spending on HIV programmes: life-skills-based HIV education is now offered in 79 per cent of the country's secondary schools; a national campaign has targeted HIV risk and alcohol abuse; and more than 25 million free male condoms (equivalent to seven condoms per male aged 15–49) are distributed each year by the public sector.

In Namibia, levels of knowledge about HIV and condom use have increased, while rates of sex before the age of 15 and sex with more than one partner in the last twelve months have decreased. Adult HIV prevalence appears to have stabilised, while HIV prevalence in young women attending antenatal clinics declined from 18 per cent in 2003 to 14 per cent in 2007.[70] National AIDS campaigns are now active in five of the eight countries that comprise the leading Group of Eight (G8)[71] industrialised nations, and these national campaigns are coordinating advocacy to ensure that HIV remains a priority for the G8.

YOUTH NETWORKS & HIV/AIDS PREVENTION

Numerous channels exist to educate young people about HIV, to ensure their access to prevention commodities and health services, and to encourage them to take steps to avoid HIV transmission. Eighty nine per cent of national governments around the world report having integrated HIV education into secondary school curricula, but far fewer have so far included HIV education in the primary school curriculum (65 per cent) or have an HIV education strategy for out-of-school young people (64 per cent). More could and should definitely be done by youth.

An example of a youth organisation active in human rights and HIV/AIDS-related topics is *IFMSA*[72] (*International Federation of Medical Students' Associations*), an independent, non-governmental and non-political federation of medical students' associations throughout the world. In particular, its *Standing Committee on Reproductive Health including AIDS* (*SCORA*) formed in 1992, driven by a strong spirit to play an active role in prevention interventions concerning HIV and sexually transmitted infections. It also aims to support people living with HIV/AIDS and to decrease stigma and discrimination[73] of such populations. One of the strengths of *IFMSA/SCORA* is that they work in partnership locally and worldwide. Through campaigns, workshops and peer education, they aim to increase awareness among medical students, as well as in the general population, of safe sexual behaviour and HIV prevention, gender equality, and women's health. Medical students from IFMSA are active in several projects and campaigns, such as World AIDS Day and International Women's Day, as well as workshops and training sessions held in different countries, from Italy to South Africa, and from Mexico to Egypt. IFMSA is officially recognised as an NGO within the United Nations' system, and acknowledged by the *WHO* as the international forum for medical students. Thus, it is not merely an organisation gathering over 1 million students from around the world – it is an active network of young people engaged in their communities to achieve a global change.

THE INTERNET'S POTENTIAL TO AMELIORATE THE IMPACT OF HIV/AIDS

Silence, taboos and myths often surround the issue of HIV/AIDS because of the associations with private and intimate behaviours. In this context, many factors may restrict young people's full enjoyment of human rights and leave them particularly exposed to HIV infection. Young people are thus at greater risk when access to clear and non-judgmental information about sexually transmitted diseases is so highly restricted.

In August 2007, *UNAIDS* held a Technical Consultation on Social Change Communication to develop a better understanding of the role of social change communication in the global response to HIV/AIDS. Social change communication involves the strategic use of advocacy, communication, and social mobilisation strategies to facilitate and/or accelerate social change. In the context of HIV/AIDS, social change communication strategies can help to alter underlying social attitudes and behaviours that contribute to HIV risk and vulnerability. Successful communication programmes combine mass media approaches, community engagement strategies, and empowerment strategies with other forms of informational and motivational communication and advocacy techniques. The goal of social change communication is to act as a catalyst for action at the individual, community, and policy levels.

Social change communication has been shown to effect significant and sustainable change in deeply-rooted practices. In 2008, *UNAIDS* developed practical guidance and technical support on social change communication for national AIDS programs.[74] According to a 2005 meta-analysis of the National Research Council,[75] five out of six youth-oriented media campaigns in various low and middle-income countries have had a measurable and proven impact on HIV-related risk behaviours. Many countries, however, are failing to make use of available channels for delivering HIV prevention information and services to young people. Whereas traditional programmes promoting information on HIV/AIDS have made extensive use of press, radio and television, road signs, private consulting in health centres and targeted information campaigns in schools, the use of the internet in particular as a means of spreading information has been largely neglected. At the time of the MDGs Declaration, the diffusion of the internet in developing countries has not been significant. For example, in 1998, in Africa, which at the time had an estimated population of 780 million, fewer than one million people had access to the internet. Of these, 80 per cent were in South Africa. Of the remaining 20 per cent, the ratio of people who had access to the internet to those who did not was 1:5000. As a point of comparison, the same ratio in Europe and the United States was 1:6.[76]

In 2000, the African people, who made up 13 per cent of the world's total population, shared just 0.3 per cent of the world's total use of the internet. Fortunately, eight years later, statistics show a dramatic increase in the diffusion of this valuable means of information for the African people. In fact, the latest estimated figures for the use of the internet in Africa are very encouraging. It is estimated that, out of a population of 955 million people, 51 million have access to the internet. This is equivalent to 3.6 per cent of the global use of the internet, a surprising increase of 1,030 per cent since 1998, second only to that in the Middle East.[77] Interestingly enough, recent surveys[78] indicate that adolescents in major urban areas[79] as well as more rural areas[80] in sub-Saharan Africa are making use of the internet to obtain health information. Hence, the potential of the internet as a conveyor of information has reached unexpected levels.

The internet has been used as a tool for medical information to reach less developed countries. However, most programmes to date have centred their efforts on conveying scientific information to academic or professional target groups, even in cooperation with scientific publishers,[81] while few initiatives have focused on the general population of internet users – consisting mostly of young people, the age group with the highest risk for HIV infection. In a recent review by Ybarra and Bull (2006), a survey of internet-based HIV prevention and intervention revealed only a handful of published studies, all of them from outside Africa.[82]

We hypothesise a strong potential for the internet to convey information on HIV/AIDS protection and the promotion of human rights among African populations. The internet-based transmission of information on HIV/AIDS has many advantages, the main one being its relatively low cost. Moreover, online information can be frequently updated and tailored by customising specific messages to different internet user groups, such as younger cyber-users. Furthermore, the internet as a means of information transmission has the advantage of being interactive. Last but not the least, it can serve as a base for stimulating users' research into further information in other health-related topics. On the negative side, however, use of the internet relies on the availability of computers and internet connections, and basic user knowledge-resources (not always widely accessible to all populations).

Strategies aimed at implementing internet-based HIV/AIDS information in African countries should, therefore, solve a two-fold challenge: the delivery of a valuable message, and the accessibility of that message to the target populations. The first point should be addressed by combining the specialised know-how of HIV/AIDS developed by the scientific community and NGOs active in the field with the expertise of professionals in online communications for conveying the target information in an effective and user-friendly way. The second point should be addressed by involving leaders and decision-makers in promoting the importance of the internet as a means of information in order to facilitate its spread. Telecommunication companies should play a major role in the implementation of this type of strategies. In particular, online access should be promoted, for instance, by offering free-of-charge internet access. In a study by Ybarra *et al* (2006),[83] 66 per cent of the interviewed Ugandan adolescents indicated that they would search for HIV/AIDS information online if access were free.

Moreover, nowadays the internet can be accessed without a computer with the use of a mobile phone. This new approach to the World Wide Web has exploded in developed countries, especially in African countries as Congo or Uganda,[84] making online access affordable even in 'non-wired' areas. This type of access could be even implemented by local enterprises with governmental or international support for their investments in exchange of their services in the form of information campaigns. As far as targets are concerned, special emphasis should be placed on increasing access to the internet by groups at high risk of HIV/AIDS infection. For example, internet access should be more available to women, who – for a variety of reasons – are more vulnerable to HIV infection. Yet, their present level of access to the internet in African countries is significantly lower compared to that of men matched in the same age range and countries.

FINAL WORDS

MDG indicators show that preventive measures are failing to keep up with the spread of the HIV/AIDS pandemic in Africa. Although key human rights (such as the right to information, the right to life and the right to health) create entitlement to care and support, most young people living with HIV/AIDS do not have the necessary access to treatment and prevention services. People living with HIV/AIDS have the potential to live vigorous, healthy and productive lives when they have access to information, treatment, care and support. Information includes knowing their rights in terms of employment, welfare, education, family life, and so on, as well as obtaining clear information about treatment and how to get it.

In the present-day global context, emphasis should be put on the role of awareness-raising campaigns and public information. Due to its tremendous development and spread over the last few years (especially in African countries), the internet has the potential for becoming a valuable tool in conveying information and help prevention of HIV/AIDS. All in all, we hypothesise an important role for campaigns of mass information through the internet, tightly connected to programmes for the diffusion of Internet connections – especially in world areas that lack it the most.

On the Legal Protection of Non-Heteronormative Identities

The Right of Homosexual People to Marry and Establish their Own Families

A Critical Review of UDHR Article 16

Haksym Chhay

Human rights are rights for all human beings. These are the freedoms and standards we must uphold to lead our lives in dignity and respect. All human rights are universal,[85] interlinked,[86] indivisible[87] and inalienable[88] (*Vienna Declaration and Programme of Action* [5] 1993). Therefore, everyone is to be entitled to their full recognition and respect as a human being regardless of race, nationality, religion, sexual orientation[89] and gender identity.[90] Yet, although the 192 member states of the United Nations have agreed to respect the principles of equal rights, respect for and self-determination of people (*UN Charter* 1945: Art. 1), severe human rights violations based on sexual orientation and gender identity still exist in the denial by the majority of national states to grant marriage and family rights to same-sex couples. This problem persists, perhaps, due to the weaknesses of Article 16 of the Universal Declaration of Human Rights (*UDHR* 1948: Art. 16), which I discuss below.

In most countries, the right to marry and establish a family is neither recognised nor respected for homosexual people. The ambiguity, incompleteness and/or misinterpretation of *UDHR* Article 16 are factors contributing to the violation of gay citizens' rights. The first paragraph of the said article states that "men and women of full age without any limitation due to race, nationality or religion, have the right to marry and to found a family. They are entitled to equal rights as to marriage, during marriage and at its dissolution". I argue that this article offers no clear explanation as to whether homosexual people are entitled to enjoy the right to marry and set up a family. Because of this gap of indeterminacy, homosexual people willing to get married are denied their right to live in dignity and respect, since same-sex marriage is not contemplated by the law.

One such example is the case of India. As a member of the United Nations, India is expected to respect the values of human rights and the self-determination of people as stated in the *UN Charter*. However, homosexual people in India cannot live in dignity, respect, peace and happiness due to the existence of an *Indian Penal (i.e. Criminal) Code*, which is still in effect. Those who violate this code are severely punished with up to ten years of imprisonment and fine or both (*Indian Penal Code*, Sec 377).

An article of news dated 11 January 2006, under the title of *India: Repeal Colonial-Era Sodomy Law* described the cruel arrest of four gay men on the charge of operating a 'gay racket' (i.e. gay business or activity) on the internet, as well as of engaging in 'unnatural' sex.

Another example of disrespect for same-sex unions comes from my native Cambodia. Article 31 of its Constitution (1993) explicitly states that it recognises and respects the *UDHR*, Covenants and other Conventions on Human Rights: "the kingdom of Cambodia shall recognise and respect human rights as stipulated in the *United Nations Charter*, the *UDHR*, the covenants and conventions related to human rights, women right's and children's rights." At the same time, however, there exists a law which bans marriage between homosexual people. This law states that "a marriage shall be prohibited to a person whose sex is the same as the other" (*Cambodian Law on Marriage and Family* 1989: Art. 6). Even though the former king of Cambodia, Norodom Sihanouk, favoured and even proposed gay marriage after watching television images of same-sex couples receiving marriage licenses in San Francisco, the *Law on Marriage and Family* still prohibits it. He added that marriage between man and man or between woman and woman should be allowed, since the government has chosen in 1993 to be a 'liberal democracy' (2004).

Nowadays, many experts have observed that human rights violations based on sexual orientation and gender identity constitute a global concern. Restrictions include denial of employment and education opportunities, and serious discrimination in relation to the enjoyment of other human rights. These violations are often compounded by experiences of other forms of violence, hatred, discrimination and exclusion. An example of these violations can be found in the work of Fraser (1997:18):

> Gays and lesbians suffer from heterosexism: the authoritative construction of norms that privilege heterosexuality. Along with these goes homophobia: the cultural devaluation of homosexuality. Their sexuality thus disparaged, homosexuals are subject to shaming, harassment, discrimination, and violence, while being denied legal rights and equal protections – all fundamentally denials of recognition. To be sure, gays and lesbians also suffer serious economic injustices; they can be summarily dismissed from paid work and are denied family-based social-welfare benefits. But far from being rooted directly in the economic structure, these derive instead from an unjust cultural–valuational structure.

Another serious challenge experienced by homosexual communities when same-sex marriage and even sodomy remain illegal is the spread of HIV/AIDS infection. Jeffrey O'Malley, the director of the United Nation's *Development Programme HIV/AIDS Group*, claims that legalising sodomy would "achieve better results regarding the protection against AIDS. Countries which protect men who have sex with men (MSM) . . . have double the rate of coverage of HIV prevention services – as much as 60 per cent"

(2008). In Cambodia, HIV prevalence at the national level dropped from 3.7 per cent in 1997 to a low of 0.9 per cent in 2006. But among men who have sex with men (MSMs), the rate remained at an uncomfortably national high of 5.1 per cent in 2006. Tony Lisle, *UNAIDS Cambodia* country coordinator, told IRIN/*PlusNews* in 2008 that "The HIV epidemic has been largely ignored among MSM". In the Philippines, according to Dr Eric Tayag, Head of the Health Department's National Epidemiology Centre, there has been a steep increase in HIV infection among SMS in the last three years. The biggest problem is that they cannot declare this epidemic in the same way it does an outbreak of dengue fever because of the "gay" stigma implicit in it (2008).

A group of human rights experts worked together at Gadjah Mada University in Yogyakarta, Indonesia, from 6 to 9 November 2006, to address the above problems of discrimination, exclusion, stigmatisation, hatred, abuse and the increasing rate of HIV infection. At the end of their meeting, they came up with the *Yogyakarta Principles on the Application of International Human Rights Laws in Relation to Sexual Orientation and Gender Identity*. Among the experts included in the drafting of the document are a former United Nations High Commissioner for Human Rights, UN independent experts, current and former members of human rights treaty bodies, as well as judges, academics and human rights defenders. The *Yogyakarta Principles* (2006) call for governments, the UN human rights system, national human rights institutions, non-governmental organisations and others to take worldwide action against violence, discrimination, exclusion and abuse due to their sexual orientation and gender identity. Regarding the right to marry and establish same-sex families, Principle 24 states that "everyone has the right to build a family, regardless of sexual orientation or gender identity. Families exist in diverse forms. No family may be subjected to discrimination on the basis of the sexual orientation or gender identity of any its members."

A practical local implementation for the promotion of the rights of homosexual people has been the work of an Indian local organisation called *TARSHI* (*Talking about Reproductive and Sexual Health Issues*). Between 11 and 16 February 2008, I was fortunate to be trained by this organisation on sexual and reproductive health and rights, including the Yogyakarta Principles. In addition, as a participant of their training session, I was brought to attend a debate between *TARSHI* resource people and policy makers. I think *TARSHI* is one of the most effective ways to raise the problems to be heard. The more frequently grievances are voiced, the more likely policy makers are to take action in favour of the aggrieved. I found this training opportunity highly inspiring. In my opinion, legalising homosexual marriage in every society will help towards eliminating stigmatisation, discrimination, exclusion and hatred attached to gay, lesbian, and other non-heterosexual citizens. And this is also one of the best solutions to deal with the sharp increase in HIV infection among these minority groups.

Last but not the least, I argue that, in order to considerably reduce discrimination, stigmatisation, exclusion, hatred and abuse due to people's actual or perceived sexual orientation and gender identity, *UDHR* Article 16 should be revised. More importantly, to avoid its ambiguity, incompleteness and/or misinterpretation, I propose that this article read "men and women of full age regardless of race, nationality, religion, sexual orientation and gender identity have the right to marry and establish a family. They are entitled to equal rights as to marriage, during marriage and at its dissolution". There should also emerge stronger commitment and participation from governments worldwide, international human rights organisations, non-governmental organisations and each one of us to make this change possible. With the participation from all stake-holders, not only will we be able to redress this grievance for non-heterosexual citizens – we will also be getting a step closer to really *valuing* human diversity in its full spectrum.

REFERENCES

The Universal Declaration of Human Rights, (1948), Art 16, Adopted and Proclaimed by General Assembly Resolution 217 A (III)

The Charter of the United Nation, (1945), Art 1, San Francisco, USA

The Constitution of the Kingdom of Cambodia, (1993), Art 31, Phnom Penh, Cambodia

The Cambodian Law on Marriage and Family, (1989), Art 6, Phnom Penh, Cambodia

The Yogyakarta Principles on the Application of International Human Rights Laws in Relation to Sexual Orientation and Gender Identity, (2006), Yogyakarta, Indonesia

Vienna Declaration and Program of Action [5], (1993), Vienna, Austria

Sihanouk, Norodom (His former majesty of the Kingdom of Cambodia), (2004), *Favoured and Proposed Gay Marriage,* http://www.utopia-asia.com/unews/article_2004_02_21_202742.htm

India: Repeal Colonial-Era Sodomy Law, (2006), http://www.hrw.org/en/news/2006/01/10/india-repeal-colonial-era-sodomy-law

Indian Penal Code, *Unnatural Offenses [Sec. 337]*

Fraser, Nancy, (1997), Justice Interruptus, *Critical Reflections on the "Postsocialist" Condition,* Routledge, New York & London

Lisle, Tony, (2008), *Sometimes I get regular women, sometimes I hire lady-boys.* http://www.nationmultimedia.com/worldhotnews/read.php?newsid=30088458

The Use of
Legal Instruments for Social Justice

The Law as a Tool for Social Change:

Land Regularisation in a Brazilian Slum

Raquel Nunes

The French philosopher Henri Lefebvre wrote that home and language are two complementary aspects of the human being.[91] However, according to the United Nations (UN), there are over 100 million homeless people[92] and 924 million people (i.e. 31.6 per cent of the world's urban population) living in slums with no adequate housing. To make matters worse, there is no evidence that this number may be decreasing. Quite the contrary – it is projected that, over the next 30 years, the number of global slum dwellers will increase to about 2 billions if no firm and concrete action is taken to halt this growth.[93]

Although inadequate housing also exists in some of the most economically developed societies, slums are a greater problem in the political South, where 43 per cent of the urban population dwells in slums.[94] The modern model of economic development that led to a rapid urbanisation has produced cities highly marked by informal settlements. So much so that today people have no access to home ownership except through mechanisms not recognised by the Law. Having no money to afford a house, some people build their own precarious, unsafe shelters in public areas, abandoned lands or areas under environmental protection, so that still they have no access to property ownership.

Slums are manifestations of urban poverty and intra-city inequality.[95] Therefore, it is not surprising that a country like Brazil, the eighth most unequal country in the world in terms of income distribution, has become notorious for its slums, or *favelas*. The most famous Brazilian movie in recent times has been *City of God*, which portrays the inhumane life of the inhabitants of a *favela* in Rio de Janeiro. According to the 2000 census, Brazil had 3,905 *favelas* across 1,542 cities, and Belo Horizonte, the city where I reside, had 101 *favelas*.[96] One of them is known as *Vila Acaba Mundo* (*End-of-the-World Village*), where I work with residents of precarious houses constantly threatened with eviction.

THE RIGHT TO HOUSING

José da Silva, who lives at *Vila Acaba Mundo*, once wrote a poem about his life in the slum:

> Humble, discriminated, ignored people [. . .] And here I am/ sitting on the floor in my shack/with my dignity in pieces./ My mind is confused/I don't know who I am/I don't know what to do/I don't know if I'm a man or a rat.[97] (Translation mine)

José da Silva's poem shows how the phenomenon of inadequate housing can contribute to breaking the dignity of a human being. This fact has been recognised by many international human rights instruments: the *Universal Declaration of Human Rights* (*UDHR*), for instance, establishes in Article 25 that everyone has the right to housing. Additionally, Article 11 of the *International Covenant on Economic, Social and Cultural Rights (ICESCR)* recognises the right of all human beings to an adequate standard of living, including adequate food, clothing and housing. *General Comment Number 4* to the *Covenant*, issued by the *UN Committee on Economic, Social and Cultural Rights* (*ESCR Committee*), emphasises that the right to housing cannot be interpreted in a narrow sense, i.e. as merely guaranteeing people a roof over their head. The right to housing entails the right to live in safety, peace and dignity. In that sense, *Comment Number 4* defines the elements of the right to housing that are objects of protection, namely: (1) legal security of tenure; (2) availability of services, materials, facilities, and infrastructure; (3) affordability; (4) habitability; (5) accessibility; (6) location and (7) cultural adequacy.

Moreover, *General Comment Number 7* specifically addresses the question of legal security of tenure after considering the significant number of reports of forced evictions received by the *ESCR Committee*. According to this Comment, forced evictions are not to result in individuals being rendered homeless or vulnerable to the violation of other human rights. In addition, with their pledge to the *UN Millennium Development Goals*, States have reinforced their commitment to the creation of cities free of inadequate housing. *Goal Number 7* (*Target 11*) sets out to promote the significant improvement of the lives of at least 100 million slum dwellers by the year 2020.

VILA ACABA MUNDO, A SLUM IN BELO HORIZONTE

As mentioned above, *Vila Acaba Mundo* is a slum located in Belo Horizonte, one of the largest cities in Brazil. As suggested by its name, the everyday life of its community is characterised by the presence of continuous violations to human rights. The average income of a family in the slum is of around US$ 224 a month and only 54 per cent of the heads of families are currently employed.[98] The small and precarious houses are built either across a contaminated creek or on the slope of a hill. Fortunately, *Vila Acaba Mundo* is located in a wealthy area of the city, which facilitates the access of its inhabitants to the municipality's public services. However, its geographical situation is also the source of one of the community's major problems: the constant threat of expulsion due to the economic interest of the real estate sector in the area.

Although the *UDHR* establishes that all human beings have the right to housing,[99] at *Vila Acaba Mundo*, people fear losing their homes to the construction of luxury apartment buildings. In such a potential scenario and having nowhere to go, slum dwellers would increase the number of homeless of the city. Alternatively, they might find a shack far away from the city centre where it is even more difficult to find a job or benefit from public services.

Despite the fact that the inhabitants of the Village have lived there for over 30 years, they do not possess legal title to the land. According to Brazilian law, if an individual has lived in an area not exceeding 250 square meters for more than 5 years, and does not possess any other real estate, they acquire property rights over this land.[100] This legal process is referred to as an *acquisitive prescription*. At *Vila Acaba Mundo,* however, the title-holders insist in displacing the residents, sometimes with the support of the Judiciary Power. Thus, the inhabitants live in constant fear of eviction and of the denial of one of the main elements of the right to housing: security of tenure.

The threat of eviction is so present in the lives of Brazilians that it has even become a *samba* in the hands of the famous composer Adoniran Barbosa:

> When the justice officer arrived/in the slum/and gave to Narciso/an eviction order/which read:/ Sir,/in 10 days/I want the entire *favela* empty/all the shacks knocked down/ it is a high order/[. . .] I'll leave/so that I won't hear the sound of the tractor/there's no problem for me/I can make do anywhere/anyhow/what I own is so little/that it fits in my pocket/but what about this people? What do we do with them? (Translation mine)[101]

The *samba* was written in 1969. Sadly enough, it could have been written today, which demonstrates the sustained and enduring violation of the rights to housing in contemporary Brazilian society.

THE *POLES OF CITIZENSHIP PROGRAMME*: A YOUTH APPROACH TO HOUSING RIGHTS

One of the mottos of political movements that fought against the Brazilian dictatorship (1964-1984) was 'Do not trust anyone over

30 years of age'. It was an aggressive way of highlighting the role of young people in pressuring for changes in society. In that spirit, the programme I work with is run by university students coordinated by a team of professors. It was created based on the idea that the university has to play an important role in tackling social problems. The *Poles of Citizenship Programme* (*Programa Pólos de Cidadania*) is an initiative of the *Federal University of Minas Gerais* (*UFMG*) which promotes teaching, research and university extension in an integrated way. With the participation of students from the most diverse areas of knowledge, the Programme aims at promoting the social integration and emancipation of social groups which have a history of marginalisation.

THE LAW AS A TOOL FOR SOCIAL CHANGE?

The *Poles Programme* began its work at *Vila Acaba Mundo* in 2004. Alongside other civil society entities, the Programme worked with the community during the process of renewal of the environmental license for the activities of two mining companies operating near the Village. The municipal legislation of Belo Horizonte establishes that, in order to obtain the renewal of their environmental licenses, mining companies must provide certain benefits to the communities established close to the location of the extraction activities. This is a way of compensating for the impact the mining causes to the local populations. In previous license renewal processes, the Village residents found themselves lacking leadership and organisation. Therefore, they were unable to demand policies with relevant effects on the improvement of the living conditions of the community (usually the mere donation of some bricks was considered enough to fulfil the requirements of the law). Nevertheless, with the support of the *Poles Programme* and of the other entities, it was possible to obtain in 2004, as a condition for the renewal of the companies' license, a whole range of measures, including the granting of funds for the land regularisation of *Vila Acaba Mundo*.

As it becomes evident, it is possible to promote social improvement through the Law. However, the Law is not enough at *Vila Acaba Mundo*; it was necessary for the Law to become integrated with a wider political movement in order to serve as a tool for social change. Only with organisation and the support of numerous civil society entities was the population able to make the provisions of the Law to have a real impact on the community. The Portuguese legal sociologist Boaventura de Sousa Santos has already observed that in order for the Law to be emancipatory, it must be used in a non-exclusive and non-autonomous way, as combined with political mobilisation.[102]

Once the license process was over, the *Poles Programme* began to work on a plan for the implementation of the land regularisation at *Vila Acaba Mundo*. As mentioned above, an *acquisitive prescription* is the legal instrument that allows an individual to acquire title to property by reason of uninterrupted possession of specified duration. Prescription has been previewed in the Brazilian judicial system for a long time. Moreover, since 2001, Brazilian Law provides for a new instrument: the *collective acquisitive prescription*, which allows people who live in urban conglomerations to go to the Judiciary collectively in order to claim property title to the lands where they have lived for more than five years.[103] Legal provisions for collective prescription are the result of decades of struggles by social movements fighting for the legal incorporation of instruments with the capacity to create a just urban order. Collective prescription is a legal instrument conceived for areas where the individualisation of each family's land is extremely complex, creating situations that the traditional individual acquisitive prescription cannot properly solve.

Notwithstanding, the proposal of promoting the land regularisation at *Vila Acaba Mundo* through judicial action was faced with resistance by the professors and some students in the *Poles Programme*, for the Judiciary is still seen with caution by organisations focused on social change. The *Poles* professors feared the conservative mentality which still prevails among judges and hinders the judicial recognition of the social function of property as enshrined in the Brazilian Constitution.[104] Other factors – such as the difficulties of the Law to deal with collective legal actions and the 'slowness' of the Brazilian Judicial Power – also contributed to the *Poles* team's decision to start searching for an alternative strategy for the land regularisation at the Village, temporarily banking on the idea of doing it through litigation.

It was possible to clearly identify within the programme the culture of litigation avoidance about which Madalena Duarte (2004) writes.[105] According to this Portuguese social scientist, social movements still do not perceive the Judiciary as an important forum for their struggle so they typically do not recourse to the courts for solutions. This statement applies to the *Poles of Citizenship Programme,* for, in order to promote the land regularisation at the Village, a different process was chosen – one that is also regulated by the Law, but which allows for stronger political action. At the moment, the *Poles Programme* is working towards the possibility of expropriating[106] the lands of the Village as the Brazilian Law allows expropriation based on social interest.[107]

The first step taken was then to demand a public meeting at the City Legislature in order to discuss the passing of a bill establishing the social interest of the lands of *Vila Acaba Mundo*. Even though the meeting took place on a weekday, the large majority of the residents were present at the gathering. This was an enormous achievement for the process of community mobilisation at the Village, which had traditionally been very difficult. The bill was presented and it already has the support of a sufficient number of councillors to pass as a municipal law. Once the law is passed, the mayor of Belo Horizonte still has to order the expropriation. It remains to be seen if popular pressure and the human rights instruments invoked will be strong enough to face the real estate sector and keep it at bay.

It is important to notice that the expropriation strategy allowed residents greater participation in the land regularisation process. Consequently, they also became more involved in other activities promoted by the *Poles Programme* at the Village. While a judicial process would mobilise only a few lawyers, the expropriation strategy created community among the residents and afforded them enhanced contact with public spaces which they had not had access to before. The demand for the public meeting was combined with the mobilisation of religious and political leadership, with the disclosure of the Village situation in the media, and with the popular resistance to judicial orders of building demolition.

The long and winding road to land regularisation at *Vila Acaba Mundo* shows that the Law can be used as a tool for social change. However, it is only a component of the struggle and must be inserted in a wider political movement, since Law interpreters tend to be very conservative and push for the maintenance of the *status quo* rather than for the transformation of an unjust society. Social movements must contribute to the counter-hegemonic use of the Law. Political mobilisation can pressure for the creation of laws that promote social justice as well as for the effective application of said laws by the Judiciary. The *Poles of Citizenship* case also comes to show that universities must be committed with society so that their students can play a fundamental role in the improvement of their local communities.

FINAL WORDS

Housing rights, as other human rights, have been widely recognised by the international community. The greater challenge that remains, however, is to stop using human rights as a rhetoric tool and to make them part of people's life. This is the merit of this UNESCO publication, which aims at portraying how youth from around the world strive to make human rights effective in their hometown. One can notice that challenges around the world can be very similar, and actions from one region can be successfully adapted to other locales.

Nevertheless, human rights must always be a collective construction, more than a selective and economically-driven imposition. That is the reason why a paramount tool necessary for the implementation of all human rights is the education of local populations, so that they are empowered to formulate their own human rights pleads. Brazilian educator Paulo Freire has taught us that people cannot be reduced to mere objects of a liberating action, performed more *over* them than *with* them. According to Freire,

> Attempting to liberate the oppressed without their reflective participation in the act of liberation is to treat them as objects which must be saved from a fire; it is to lead them into the populist pitfall and make them become a mass that can be manipulated.[108] (Translation mine)

Emancipation is a human phenomenon which aims at building subjects and citizens. Therefore, there can be no emancipation in a process that treats people as semi-humans or things, unable to think and act for themselves. There is no emancipation without participation, so it is not possible to liberate someone using mechanisms of domestication.

REFERENCES

Constituição Federal de 1988 (Brazil)

Duarte Madalena, 2004, "Novas e Velhas Formas de Protesto: o Potencial Emancipatório da Lei nas Lutas dos Movimentos Sociais." *Oficina do CES*, 210, Centro de Estudos Sociais, Coimbra

Freire Paulo, 2005, *Pedagogia do Oprimido*, Paz e Terra, Rio de Janeiro

Instituto Brasileiro de Geografia e Estatística (IBGE), 2001, *Census of 2000* <http://www.ibge.gov.br>

Lefebvre Henri, 1999, *A Revolução Urbana*, Belo Horizonte: Editora UFMG

Lei No. 10.257, de 10 de julho de 2001, DOU de 11.07.2001, Art. 10 (Brazil)

UN GAOR, 43rd Sess., Supplement n. 8, addendum, UN Doc. A/43/8/Add.1

UN-HABITAT, 2003, *The Challenge of Slums:* Global Report on Human Settlements, UN Human Settlements Programme, Earthscan Publications, London and Sterling

Santos, Boaventura de Sousa, 2002, "Can Law Be Emancipatory?" *Red Latino Americana de Antropología-Jurídica*, 10 July 2008 <http://www.geocities.com/relaju/souzasantos.htm>

Locating the Individual in the Universal Declaration of Human Rights

Aheli Purkayastha

All too often in history, we see countries move forward after severe human rights violations without adequately addressing the social traumas that resulted from such acts. While these countries regularly announce their commitment to 'human right', they often fail to take active steps in ensuring such fundamental rights. Instead, these countries rely on individuals to initiate different movements and actions. This paper examines how individuals can effect change and ensure the protection of human rights at a local and global level.

THE HUMAN RIGHTS BACKGROUND

The *Universal Declaration of Human Rights* (*UDHR*) outlines the importance of individual action in effecting change at a local and global level. In order to respond to the severe, often-state sponsored brutalities – such as genocides, holocausts, wars, and colonialism, the *UDHR* was created in the aftermath of World War II. The *UDHR* is a declaration of universal principles that set a precedent for understanding the value of individual human beings around the world. Each of the thirty separate, yet highly integrated, articles expresses the belief in the inherent value of each person and the inalienable rights of all citizens of the world as the foundations of freedom, peace, and justice.

As the goal of the *UDHR* was to address the failures of states to protect individual human rights, the *UDHR* emphasises the importance of protecting human rights from both an individual and global level. First, the *UDHR* suggests that human beings are connected in fundamental ways and that they cannot function as isolated being or fragmentary nations, ethnicities or other social identities. Instead, the *UDHR* asserts that human beings must develop together, through the cultivation of multiple bonds and ties. Secondly, *UDHR* Article 1 asserts that *all* human beings are born free and equal in dignity and rights, and that they should act towards one another in a 'spirit of brotherhood'.[109] Thus freedom and dignity are inherent in *individual* human beings, rather than in projects of larger social and political institutions.

RESTORING JUSTICE

In continuing with this vision of Universal Human Rights, activists and scholars have articulated a specific *way* of addressing human rights violations by utilising individuals' rights to recognise the need to move forward from situations of confrontation. This form of *Restorative Justice* addresses issues of humanity and emphasises that individuals are affected by human rights violations. The ideas found in Article 1 are clearly embodied in the notion of *restorative justice,* which targets the individual, rather than the state, in the rebuilding process.

Restorative Justice emphasises involving all stakeholders and transforming the traditional relationships between communities and their governments in responding to human rights violations.[110] The goal of restorative justice, according to the Suffolk University Centre, is to "engage those who are harmed, wrongdoers, and their affected communities in search of solutions that promote repair, reconciliation and the rebuilding of relationships".[111] This idea is grounded in the same notion perpetuated by Article 1, i.e. in the idea of a common humanity and that of respecting that each one enjoys one's right to equality and protection of the law, as well as the right to freedom of movement, opinion, expression, conscience and religion, and the right to assemble peacefully.

It is important to understand that, in order to effect change and address issues of human rights violations, it is important to first begin with the people involved in each conflict. It is pointless to say that states are to blame because states are made up of individuals. *Restorative Justice* addresses this idea by attempting to re-build relationships. As with the case of the South African *Truth and Reconciliation Commission (1992),* individuals may come forward to a court-like body to give a testimony on their experience. This process recognises that change must be developed and savoured through multiple bonds and ties rather than being implemented top-down by organisations that might be far removed from the daily lives of individuals. What is remarkable about the *Truth and Reconciliation Commission* is the simplicity of the idea: to offer a space where people can go to have their stories heard and documented. The act of going there in itself initiates the restorative justice process. Equally important is that it allows people a chance to move on without being tied down by the hurts and hatreds that typified the conflicto.

Through my work as a social activist, I have grown to value this perspective. At a local level, when people are harmed by racist acts or women are victims of violence, it is important to address the wrong, move beyond it, *and* find ways to change the situation. Restorative justice principles can be very important here. Such social change can only begin through human contact. It is important to keep working with all the stake-holders to at least address the hurts and harms openly. The idea is to help people move beyond a position where cumulative harms severely restrict their human lives. Following the principles of restorative justice, to achieve longer-term effects, we have to also work to change the people who constitute the culture and institutional arrangements that allowed the harm to happen in the first place. Restorative justice requires us to listen to all voices in a local 'post-conflict' situation; otherwise, the silence of those affected will override the change desired. While we may not always reach this ideal, it is important to keep working towards it if we truly believe in promoting societies where human rights of all are valued.

The *UDHR*[112] was meant as a declaration of universal principles for countries to follow, rather than a set of narrowly-defined legal rules. These principles are, in turn, easily adaptable to all types of situations, from the apartheid system to college campus happenings. I believe *UDHR* is not simply about international and national-level aspirations and changes, it is very much a blue print for our everyday living.

FINAL WORDS

Ultimately, every act of social change begins through human interaction. Individuals must reach out to other individuals, in their community or across the world, in order to raise awareness of a specific issue. These interactions can take place in many different ways – whether through informal networks or through formal organisations.[113] The problem is that we no longer look at the role of the individual citizen and are often too concerned with larger, more macro-level of politics. If we cannot value the role of the individual citizen, and their capacity for change, we can no longer address modern-day problems – such as genocides, global warming, or other large-scale global issues.

REFERENCES

Abraham Margaret, 2000, *Speaking the Unspeakable*, Rutgers University Press, New Brunswick

Glenn, Evelyn Nakano, 2002, *Unequal Freedoms*, Harvard University Press, Cambridge, MA

Lauren Paul, 2000, "Proclaiming a Vision" in: *The Evolution of International Human Rights*, University of Pennsylvania Press, Philadelphia

Nandy Ashis, 1994, The *Illegitimacy of Nationalism*, Oxford University Press, New Delhi

Purkayastha Bandana, 2002, "Non-cooperation as a Means of Peaceful Conflict Resolution: Cases from India" *Forum International*, 22:267-292, Germany

Purkayastha Bandana, 2003, "Contesting the Boundaries of Home and the World: Tagore and the Construction of Citizenship" in: Patrick Colm Hogan and Lalita Pandit (Ed) *Rabindranath Tagore at the End of the Millennium: Questions of Gender, Nation, Science and Tradition*, Farleigh Dickenson Press, Madison and Associated University Press, London, p.49-64

Are the UN Millennium Development Goals the Solution to World Problems?

Beatriz Borges Urrutia

Our world has many problems: hunger, poverty, wars, epidemics, national conflicts, discrimination, drug trafficking, pollution, global warming and crimes are just some of them. It is assumed that governments must work on a daily basis to solve all these complex problems which characterise our contemporary lives. To that end, countries must use all their resources in the most efficient way possible, yet sometimes resources turn out to be scarce. As we all know, most problems are common to many countries, which is why efforts to find common solutions are a good direction to take. In today's global context, international organisations created by groups of countries are attempting to do their best to join efforts and ideas to help solving common global problems. Although sharing difficult circumstances and working together to find solutions by proposing common goals are not easy tasks, they are certainly worth the effort. Actually, finding common solutions entails a complex process that involves many factors and the need for a multiplicity of strategies.

In addition to the complexity of global issues and despite organised efforts to find solutions to common problems, international organisations such as the United Nations are sometimes criticised for their lack of familiarity with the realities of the countries they seek to help and their ensuing solutions which remain distant to the grassroots problems. In this context, the *Millennium Development Goals* (*MDGs*) – i.e. eight goals that all 191 member countries of the United Nations have agreed to achieve by 2015 – emerged. This initiative born in 2000 represents an interesting effort by the United Nations to point out over the common and difficult problems of the humanities and a good way to solve them together as an international community. Yet . . . are the *MDGs* the solution to today's global problems? And, what can each of us do to support this work? In this paper, I offer a personal reflection on these questions in order to encourage readers to become increasingly involved in a unique opportunity to change the world being part of the MDGs' movement.

In the *Millennium Declaration* (2000), are collected eight goals relating to the achievement of poverty eradication, universal primary education, gender equality, child and maternal mortality decrease, HIV/AIDS reduction, and environmental sustainability. Each goal is, in turn, subdivided into a series of 18 goals, measurable through 48 specific indicators. For the first time in human history, the international development agenda set a date for reaching concrete and measurable goals. Nevertheless, reaching those goals is not a simple task. Personally, I believe in two things that can help reach the goals established in the *MDGs*, namely: Human Rights and Public Policy.

When we talk about the *MDGs*, we talk about both Public Policy and Human Rights. These are the platforms where the MDGs are based, so it is where governments and civil society should focus ther work. The peculiarity of these two concepts lies in their different understandings but closed relationship. No right can be guaranteed if it does not have a public policy that supports it.

Firstly, governments should be working to fulfil their obligations set in the international human rights treaties and in their own constitutions. They must fulfil their obligations of not violating human rights (i.e. for instance, not by killing or torturing people), but they also need to act towards the fulfilment of the obligation to promote Human Rights (i.e. implementing reforms in their legislation or developing public programs). They should not focus only on protecting Human Rights: they should focus on making Human Rights become an everyday fact for people. Governments must develop an agenda for social, economic and cultural rights in order to make the latter a reality for their citizens. On the other hand, civil society must know its rights and be involved in the demand for them. As civil society, we must know the *MDGs* and work together with government to achieve these goals.

Secondly, governments must work with all the available resources in an effective way to implement efficient public policies geared at improving people's quality of life. Public policies are to be designed with governments' economic resources and include mechanisms of ethical accountability for society's benefit. Knowing our rights and understanding the problems and solutions posed by the *MDGs*, we can accelerate the process of achieving of these goals and monitoring the work of governments.

However, the MDGs have sometimes been critiqued as unfair or overambitious. Nevertheless, it should be borne in mind that the MDGs constitute/represent a universal effort to solve humanity's common problems around the world. Right now, the objectives are the main targets on the agenda of the UN agencies, international cooperation organisations, NGOs and official agencies, becoming a global movement where there are many actors involved. It is in this context that civil society should take advantage of that and work towards the same objectives that are ultimately being looked into for improving global problems.

It is my contention that it is important to ask: Will the MDGs make the world better in 2015? This is a difficult question to answer, but it is important that our future depends on the answer. I believe it will be helpful and also I have a good feeling about it. We as a race have many good prospects on our side and also many others against us. For example, the fact that the governments present substantial results on the progress achieved in regard to the MDGs is a good sign that there is a work, a political will and commitment.

Still, if we all get involved in the *MDGs* movement, things will start improving because it is not just a government job – it is a job for all citizens to take on. We need to do all in our power to improve the present global situation and complain to governments each time that they do not protect our rights and fight for everybody's well-being. Yet, governments are not the only ones that must work on this. All we must do for our share. In that respect, I would like to share a short story that a very close friend of mine, a great political leader from my motherland of Venezuela who died fighting for justice few months ago, once told me.

His story talks about a man who was walking along the beach shore, feeling depressed. He felt like his life was of no worth any longer. The night before, there had been such a big storm on the beach that all the starfish were now on the sand by the sea-line. Without water, they would all die. But the man thought that he could not stand there doing nothing to help them – so he felt even worse. He then found a little boy on the way who was doing his best to save all the starfish: he was picking one at a time and throwing it back into the sea. When the man saw this, he felt humbled. He could not understand why this little boy was doing that. So he approached the boy and with a strong voice asked: "Why are you doing this? Can't you see that you can't save them all? There are too many! Don't you waste your time only saving just a few!" The boy stopped for a minute, looked at the man, and said: "Maybe you are right," taking another starfish in his hands. "But at least this one will be saved."

Are the *UN Millennium Development Goals* the solution to solve world's problems? As mentioned previously, there are many problems out there and the solutions are very complex. But as individuals and organisations, we should not think of the small size of the things that we can do – we should rather think of the big impact that those small things can have on our lives and on that of others. This is the key to becoming involved in a universal movement such as the *MGDs* movement. You never know who or when the small things that you do will help people in this world. For this reason, becoming a part of the United Nations' *MDGs* movement is a great opportunity to start effecting positive change. There are indeed many things that each one of us can do to make real changes in our world. Do not let the chance pass you by – start saving your own starfish!

Human Rights Education

Hope for a Brighter Future

Nerina Maqueira

I come from a middle-class Argentine family. When I was a child, my parents could afford to send me to a private school. All my classmates lived in the same neighbourhood and were taken to school by their parents, who also attended parent-teacher meetings and helped them do the homework after school every day. So did my parents. For me, the world was all about cute clothes, clean school uniforms, vacations on the beach, loving and caring mummies and supportive daddies.

When I finished high school, I went to college for Educational Psychology, a programme that is only offered in a few countries. In the case of Argentina, the programme is only offered in a few private institutions. So once again, I found myself in a middle-class context. To us, it was all too common to talk about credit cards, vacations overseas, and the possibility of studying in Europe or the USA. After obtaining my first degree, I decided to become an English teacher and so applied to graduate school for a BA in TESOL. And once again, the choice was a private institute. So many years of private environments had made me unaware of the existence of a different world beyond the clean walls that, one way or another, had always offered me shelter from the harder reality out there.

Two years ago, I decided to apply for a job in a public school for a change. In fact, even when it makes me feel absolutely embarrassed, I have to admit that I did it out of interest. I just needed a year-round salary and paid vacations. Today, however, after having been in touch with this 'other world', I feel I would be willing to work there for free. In Argentina, middle and upper-class children go to private schools, whereas children and teenagers from disadvantaged backgrounds attend public institutions. I was hired in a public school to teach English to freshmen twice a week. In 'my world', teenagers who are thirteen are freshmen, fourteen-year-olds are sophomores, and so on till they graduate at age seventeen and start college at age eighteen.[114] That is the usual way.

As soon as I started working in the public school, I found out that my 24-student class ranged in age from 13 to 16. Almost half were repeating students, i.e. they were being made to retake their freshman year for a first or even for a second time. In spite of their differences in physical, mental or sexual development, the students all shared the same classroom. This situation – unfortunately very common in Argentine public schools – means that the younger students are exposed to comments and situations that they may not be ready to experience at their age. The unspoken code is quite clear: the most naïve, shy and immature of the class will either be forced to mature within the first two months in high school, or be cruelly bullied or made fun of.

EDUCATION AND SOCIAL CLASS IN CONTEMPORARY ARGENTINA

It is relatively easy to study and to make academic progress when one's basic needs are covered, i.e. when one's parents are supportive, when dialogue in the family is a possibility, when money is not an issue every day of one's lives . . . That, however, is not the case for my students. Sometimes, life is so cruel to them that they cannot even feel hopeful about the possibility of ever improving their lives. To begin with, their living conditions are far from ideal. Most of them live in very poor neighbourhoods or even shanty towns. Their houses are usually built in corrugated iron, making their homes bitterly cold in the winter while extremely hot in the summertime.

At home, they share very small bedrooms with their six or seven siblings, or even with adults who do not necessarily belong to their families. Domestic overcrowding very frequently leads to situations of abuse that range from psychological violence to physical abuse or rape. In such contexts, elder brothers, step-fathers, uncles and neighbours, for instances, represent real threats to girls (and occasionally, boys) of all ages.

To make matters worse, some of the students in the school do not live with their parents because, as the latter have several children to feed, they tend to send the older ones to live elsewhere. Because of the areas and conditions these children live in, the police easily view them as suspicious and thus are likely to detain them for background checks. Alcoholism and addiction to all types of drugs are also very common in deprived areas. Both may cause other problems, which, in turn, might increase the vicious circle of addiction. Some of these include increased marginalisation, higher crime rates to afford drugs and alcohol, family violence (especially due to drunken parenting and family battering), infant mortality, and alcohol-related conditions (such as cirrhosis, nervous disorders, and lung cancer)

SCHOOL AS A SAFE HAVEN?

The school I work at is located in a major neighbourhood in Buenos Aires city, while the shanty towns where my students live are in the city outskirts. This means that students need to commute by bus or train to get to the school. Most of them would do so on their own. Just to mention some of the dangers of the typical commute, in Argentina public transportation (especially trains) are in really poor condition, making them very unsafe and likely scenarios of robbery and sexual harassment.

For these young students, the school should be a place for protection and belonging which they may not be able to get elsewhere. Yet, it is not. Students continuously get low grades, frequently bunk off class, have behavioural issues, or are made fun of by their peers. In other words, the school experience mostly provides them with a total sense of personal failure. In such a context, it is very difficult for teachers to actually *teach* any course to these students—especially a foreign language. English, in particular, is very hard for us to teach because students are not in contact with the language at their homes and thus feel that it is too aloof to be of any use to them.

Their economic and social situation precludes them from the vision that one day, with effort and a bit of luck, they might be able to travel abroad or work for an international company. Their hard lives have numbed them to any kind of hope, so much so that most of them cannot see the advantage of attaining a high level of education. The following real-life stories reflect the way in which these teenagers' disadvantaged backgrounds may prevent them from engaging in formal education to improve their lives. Nicknames have been used for confidentiality purposes.

Isabel's Story

Isabel is fifteen years old. She was born in a province in the north of Argentina – 1,100 kilometres from Buenos Aires. When she finished elementary school in her small hometown, she gave up school due to personal issues that prevented her from furthering her studies. Two years later, she managed to move to Buenos Aires and started her secondary education.

In her first term, Isabel got very low grades in almost all the subjects. When I talked to her, she told me that she needed some time to adapt to school again. The next term, her marks were very good, not only in English but in the other subjects as well. I even made a point of her improvement in front of her classmates and told them that she was a good example of hard work, determination and responsibility. I was really moved by her case and felt very proud of her. However, during her third trimester, Isabel left school. She just went missing overnight. Her friends told me that she had gone back to her hometown. They also said that, even though her mother lived in Buenos Aires, Isabel had been living with her boyfriend in a different place for quite some time.

One day, he got more violent than usual and hit her. He kicked her out of the place they shared. As she had nowhere to go, she had to leave the city and go back to her province.

Gabriela's Story

At the end of the school term last year, Gabriela (14) had to sit for several final exams given that she had flunked most of her freshman classes.[115] She never showed up to her English final examination. Two days later, we met and she told me that she had missed the examination because she had had to take her brother's girlfriend (who was also 14) to have an abortion performed. That was the second time that her brother had made his girlfriend pregnant. So this was her second abortion. She did not mention how they got the money for the first abortion. But for the second intervention, Gabriela and her brother had sold their digital camera and told their father that somebody had stolen it at a concert. Gabriela is now doing her freshman year for a third time.

Vicky's Story

Vicky is a 15-year-old girl who lives in a shanty town – or rather, she *used to* live in one. According to what she once said, her father was a drug dealer. Vicky had not been to school for the last three weeks. Her classmates told me that her boyfriend was a robber and a drug addict. Apparently, he had learnt that the police was about to catch him and he ran away. Nobody knows if Vicky was forced to go with him or if she did it out of her own choice. Whatever the case might have been, the fact is that she has dropped out of school and is now roaming the streets with an older teenager who is wanted by the police.

THE HUMAN RIGHTS FRAMEWORK

Given that these and similar kinds of problems faced by children and adolescents with disadvantaged backgrounds affect their personal fulfilment and sense of dignity, they should ideally be considered from a human rights perspective. The reality is that those in underprivileged conditions, on a daily basis, face situations diametrically opposed to the wishes and aspirations written into the documents such as the *Universal Declaration of Human Rights* (*UDHR*), the *International Covenant on Economic, Social and Cultural Rights*, or the *Convention against Discrimination in Education*.

Article 25 of the *UDHR*, for instance, states that:

> (1) Everyone has the right to a standard of living adequate for the health and well-being of himself and of his family, including food, clothing, housing and medical care and necessary social services, and the right to security in the event of unemployment, sickness, disability, widowhood, old age or other lack of livelihood in circumstances beyond his control.
>
> (2) Motherhood and childhood are entitled to special care and assistance. All children, whether born in or out of wedlock, shall enjoy the same social protection.

Certainly, adolescents of disadvantaged backgrounds lack a standard of living adequate to their well-being in many respects. Similarly, the *International Covenant on Economic, Social and Cultural Rights* provides the most comprehensive article on the right to health in international human rights law. Article 12.1 recognises "the right of everyone to the enjoyment of the highest attainable standard of physical and mental health". Health is a fundamental human right which is indispensable for the exercise of other human rights. Every human being is entitled to the enjoyment of the highest attainable standards of health conducive to a dignified and dignifying life.

The right to health embraces a wide range of socio-economic factors that promote conditions under which people can lead a healthy life. The right extends to the underlying determinants of health, such as food and nutrition, housing, access to safe running water, gas, electricity and adequate sanitation, healthy working conditions and a healthy environment. Taking this comprehensive article into account, it is important to notice that children and teenagers of disadvantaged backgrounds lack most of the rights covered in its clauses.

Similarly, poor people often cannot afford to have the four necessary daily meals. In fact, the only food they may get at times is that which they are provided at school, which consists of a sandwich and a muffin. At home, what they eat frequently lacks nutritional value and its only purpose is to fill up their stomachs. They may even eat what other people throw away, i.e. leftovers picked out of trash cans. In other words, many lower-class teenagers and children are severely under and malnourished.

To add insult to injury, their families for the most part live in small, uncomfortable shanty houses in very deprived areas. Most of them are shacks made out of corrugated iron sheets and do not even have cement floors. Neither do they have running water, which increases their likelihood of contracting a number of illnesses, such as severe diarrhoea, which may put their lives at serious risk.

In terms of employment, many of these teenagers and children have to work in order to help their parents bringing some money into their households. Young people scavenge for cardboard boxes in the streets to then sell them out for a few coins. Their workplace is among trash bags and animal faeces. That is, both the living and working environments are, for the most part, filthy, insecure and unhealthy. Unhealthy environments can cause the emergence of poverty-related diseases, such as cholera, leprosy or yellow fever, to mention only a few. Likewise, the appearance of tumours and malformations are also frequent in underprivileged population due to environmental pollution.

THE EFFECTS OF SOCIAL PROBLEMS ON EDUCATION

In Argentina, education is free and compulsory in the elementary level. The problem is that disadvantaged children and teenagers usually experience a number of situations unrelated to education that, in one way or the other, may hinder their formal education. Unfortunately, education is not always directed towards overall development of students' personalities, but rather towards learning facts, dates or figures. This approach casts aside the importance of helping children and teenagers develop strong moral values and tender, generous hearts.

LOOKING FORWARD AS A YOUTH

Unfortunately, due to the current world economic crisis and to Argentina's never-ending financial depression, I can only see the problem of young students of underprivileged background getting worse and worse. I really do not think that the problem will be tackled effectively at a global level in the short-to-medium term. However, in small areas, the problem can be more successfully dealt with in more creative ways, thanks to the efforts and commitment of young activists.

In Payatas, Philippines, for instance, Arcie Mallari (see his own essay in this collection) has founded a project called *Silid Aralan Inc* (*Learning Room*). Arcie (27, economist) wanted to have a personal immersion experience in the poorest area of the city where he lives, so he spent some time living in a local dumpsite, among children who sorted out garbage to make a living out of it. *Silild Aralan* and their partners started serving forty children a year ago and are now planning to serve a total of 167 kids next academic year. They seek to 1) motivate; 2) escalate; 3) integrate; 4) create and 5) celebrate education for all.

A VIABLE SOLUTION?

From an economic viewpoint, there may be no possible solution to the problem of education and poverty, for, historically, local governments have proved highly ineffective in eradicating poverty and thinking in ways that will favour the underprivileged for a change. Many things should be done to improve the lives of underprivileged children and teenagers. On the other hand, from an educational perspective, there are certain things that can be done to help lower-class youth change their mindsets about themselves as well as their own realities.

It is my opinion that the education offered at school should go beyond the specific academic subjects. Teachers should be able to deliver much more than information. A lesson may be interrupted because two students start yelling at each other or a group of students start laughing at an individual. The teasing can be on the basis of origin, citizenship, physical features, lack of skills, manner of speaking, or many other aspects. This leads to a climate of restrained violence. When it is impossible to teach a structure or a grammatical rule, when it is impossible to make the students remember the starting date of the WWI, the teachers should definitely try to educate them in other issues such as tolerance and respect for others. On certain occasions, there emerge many problems in the classroom which have nothing to do with learning contents.

It is usually very difficult to deal with conflicts once they surface. In fact, the easiest way to deal with conflicts is by preventing them from emerging at all. This can be done by teaching students to be accepting, to learn from differences, to respect other cultures, to be open-minded towards people who do not wish to share their views, thoughts or customs. Education can and must be the key to a better future. The education imparted to these underprivileged children and teenagers should, by all means, include the teaching of Human Rights. Only people who are aware of their rights can fight for them to be respected. Human Rights Education is the key to any kind of education.

FINAL WORDS: ANDY'S STORY AS AN INSPIRATION FOR TEACHERS

Andy (16) is a freshman in the school where I work. He has had a hard life. He was born in 1992, the youngest of five siblings in a lower-middle class family. His father has never held permanent employment, having worked alternately as a custodian, a taxicab driver, and a door-to-door salesman. His mother used to run/ manage a small sweet shop.

When Andy was five years old, his mother died of a heart attack. For the next two to three years, his father took care of his five children. When it became too difficult for him to keep doing this alone, Andy's aunt offered all of them to live with her. When Andy was twelve, his father died of lung cancer and his aunt became his only support since, after his father's death, his elder brothers went away. Shortly after his father had died, Andy developed a glaucoma that turned into retinal damage. As a result, he had to undergo vision surgery. The operation was partially successful: he now suffers from limited vision in his right eye.

Andy's performance in primary school was quite weak. He had to re-do both 4th and 6th grades. He walked to school by himself because his aunt worked the whole day. When he was in 4th grade, he was repeatedly robbed and hit by people on his way to school. So his aunt decided to find another school for him. However, 'safe schools' are nowhere near where they live, so two years ago Andy had to start commuting into Buenos Aires city – the daily commute into and out of town is two hours by bus each way.

Andy is tall and well-built. He is relatively big for his age and does not fit into the 'ideal' physical model pushed by the media. His schoolmates often call him names like 'tank' and tease him because of his size. Whatever he does, they laugh at him. Every day, when he comes back from school, he washes his shabby clothes – the same ones he will be wearing the next day – and prepares himself something to eat, because his aunt works till late.

At the beginning of the year, when I first met the incoming cohort, I was taken aback by the fact that almost half of the students were retaking the class for a second or even a third time. Because of their academic records, I soon realised that teaching them all the contents of the programme was out of the question. Teaching them values, good behaviour, respect for the others and the benefits of working hard seemed a much more solid choice. Unfortunately, however, the year did not go as planned. Most of them were really bad at learning contents and they did not do better in terms of behaviour, values, non-discrimination or personal efforts. Many times I thought about sliding back into my traditional role as a teacher, explaining concepts without taking into consideration any other aspect of the students. But right when I was feeling really disappointed, I started noticing that one of them was beginning to change his attitude. He started to show interest, not only in the English language itself, but also in all the other non-academic messages I was trying to put across. He started to feel motivated; he asked for the meaning of new words; he attended extra lessons to improve his grades; he took a front seat instead of being at the back with those students who misbehaved; he asked his mates to be quiet during the lessons; and, most importantly, he started to think of the future.

That student was Andy. Andy, who in spite of his sad, painful reality, had decided to make a change for himself; had decided to work hard in an attempt to improve his life and enhance his future. In 2007, he had flunked out of nine subjects. This year he has passed all of them. Andy has really become my inspiration. Right when I was feeling the urge to quit my job at the school, right when the laziness I could sense in my other students was beginning to jeopardise my own professional and personal faith, Andy was there to remind me that, no matter how many people may shrug off my message of hope, only one listener can make it all worthwhile. Just one person – Andy in my case – can make anyone reconsider that there *is* actually hope for a brighter future. Each of us can change the world, one person at a time.

Peace Education as a Tool for the Reinforcement of Human Rights and Fundamental Freedoms

Nermine Mounir

Human rights affect every aspect of our lives. Indeed, violations of human rights lie at the root of almost every problem in the world today: violence, poverty, globalisation, the environment, economic inequality, and lawlessness. Not to mention the wars and conflicts which are destroying parts of the globe. Although human rights, in their original conception, were broadly confined to the civil and political spheres, it is now acknowledged that they must also embrace social, cultural, and economic issues as well. Today, people even speak of a third generation of human rights that takes into account collective rights and issues concerning future generations of humankind.

The *Universal Declaration of Human Rights* (*UDHR*) is based on the assumption that, to ensure world peace, human rights must be protected. Respect for human rights encourages individuals, groups, and corporate entities such as the state, to avoid inflicting intentional, unnecessary harm to any human being. War itself is a systematic assault on human rights. Standards of living are reduced, food and material shortages are common, people are terrorised, freedom is minimised, and typically the rights of women are systematically violated.

Drawing on my own experience, I will highlight throughout this essay how peace education can promote respect of and value for human rights among individuals and societies out of a need for peace. Peace education can provide a space for exploration of the self, the other, the underlying fears and stereotypes, lacking skills, missing positive values, alternative. It also seeks to create a space for sincere human interactions, a space of learning and growth that will hopefully bring us a little more openness, a little more tolerance, a little less violence, and little more peace with ourselves and with others. In other words, it aims to develop spaces where people can safely explore diversity as valuable attitudes and promote non-violent conflict resolution skills.

PEACE EDUCATION

Article 26 of the *Universal Declaration of Human Rights* (*UDHR*) states that "Education shall be directed to the full development of the human personality and to the strengthening of respect for human rights and fundamental freedoms. It shall promote understanding, tolerance and friendship among all nations, racial or religious groups, and shall further the activities of the United Nations for the maintenance of peace". Peace education has thus developed as a means to achieve these goals. Peace education encompasses the key concepts of education and peace.

While it is possible to define *education* as a process of systematic institutionalised transmission of knowledge and skills, as well as of basic values and norms that are accepted in a certain society, the concept of *peace* is less clearly defined. John Galtung makes an important distinction between positive and negative peace. *Negative peace* is defined as the absence of large-scale physical violence, i.e. lack of the condition of war. *Positive peace*, on the other hand, goes beyond the mere absence of war: it states that peace can only be addressed by means of a search for justice and by understanding structural forms of exploitation and injustice. Peace is a condition of security and trust in which each individual can flourish to his or her own full potential and offer society the full measure of his or her talents and abilities.

Accordingly, peace education may be defined as an interdisciplinary area of education whose goal is institutionalised and non-institutionalised teaching about peace and for peace. Peace education aims to help students acquire skills for non-violent conflict resolution for active and responsible action in the society . . . Its aim is to prevent a violent conflict prior to its occurrence by educating individuals and society for a peaceful existence on the basis of non-violence, tolerance, equality, respect for differences, and social justice.

Therefore, peace education curricula should push students to consider how war reduces human dignity, obstructs rights to security of person and bodily integrity, destroys ecological systems, and belittles the value of human life. Conceptualising non-violent alternatives to armed conflicts (such as civil disobedience and other possibilities for the fulfilment of human rights) are important components of peace education.

RATIONALE FOR PEACE EDUCATION

In his book *Peace Education: Exploring Ethical and Philosophical Foundations* (2008), James Page explored some possible ethical – philosophical foundations that provide a rationale for peace education through an examination of five specific ethical traditions, namely: (1) *virtue ethics*, whereby peace may be interpreted as a virtue, and/or virtue is interpreted as peacefulness, and peace education as education in that virtue; (2) *consequentialist ethics*, whereby peace education may be interpreted as education regarding the consequences of our action and inaction, both as individuals and collectivities; (3) *conservative political ethics*, whereby peace education may be interpreted as emphasising the importance of the evolution of social institutions and the importance of ordered and lawful social change; (4) *aesthetic ethics*, whereby peace may be interpreted as something beautiful and valuable in itself, and peace education as emphasising the importance of that beauty and value; and (5) *the ethics of care*, whereby care may be interpreted as a core element in peace, and peace education as encouraging trust and engagement with the other. He concludes that each of these traditions provides only a partial basis for peace education, and that ultimately a holistic and integrative understanding is required to promote a culture of peace.

VALUES INCORPORATED IN PEACE EDUCATION

Peace education is based on a philosophy that teaches *non-violence, love, compassion, trust, fairness, cooperation, respect,* and reverence for the human family and all life on our planet . . . It also involves respect for others regardless of race, gender, age, nationality, class, sexuality, appearance, political or religious belief, physical or mental ability. Other characteristics include empathy (i.e. a willingness to understand the views of others from their standpoint); a belief through which individuals and groups can attain positive change; appreciation of and respect for diversity; self-esteem (i.e. accepting one's intrinsic value and self-worth); commitment to social justice, equity and non-violence; concern for the environment and understanding of our place in the eco-system; and commitment to equality.

KNOWLEDGE INCORPORATED IN PEACE EDUCATION

At the core of the knowledge that peace education imparts lies the understanding of group dynamics. Human beings live in groups: families, hunting groups, tribes, villages, cities, castes, guilds, armies, trade unions, political parties, classes (school and social), empires, nation states, confederations, international organisations, gender groups, and humankind – to name but a few. Peace education should enable us to understand the interaction between the group and the individual: How does the group form of the individuals? How does the group place the individuals in certain positions? How may the individual influence the group? It should also focus on creating awareness of the self and how our personal and collective experiences shape our choices and values, which in turn help us understand diversity, its origins, and implications. In addition, peace education can involve knowledge

bring us to a little more openness, a little more tolerance, a little less violence, and little more peace with ourselves and with others . . .

THE MISRIYATI PEACE EDUCATION PROGRAMME—AN EGYPTIAN YOUTH INITIATIVE

Inspiration

This project was inspired in early 2004 by discussions about the fish and shark car stickers' phenomenon in Egypt. The Christians started posting fish stickers on their cars, and Muslims posting shark stickers. The phenomenon illustrated the growing intolerance among the different components of Egyptian society: religions, social classes and cultural groups, which manifested in the increasing incidents of religious tension, growing sectarian isolation, and the difficult communication among the different social classes and subcultures.

Misryati not only focuses on creating public awareness on intolerance in society, but also on creating self-awareness and understanding of how behaviour and action can be changed in order to benefit oneself and the society. The main purpose of Misryati is to create personal transformation: "We work on human beings to create self awareness and awareness on the social reality, which will then help the individual transform his own surrounding."

The Misriyati Vision

Egyptian society knowing about principles of peaceful living and non-violent ways of dealing with conflicts, and having the possibility of applying those principles in their daily lives.

The Misriyati Mission

- Providing the knowledge
- Creating the success stories, the examples and models
- Creating the space and community for peaceful living

The Misriyati programme aims at creating these spaces where people can safely explore diversity as a value, the diversity within the Egyptian society, and learning the skills of dealing with conflicts in a non-violent way . . . discovering our own underlying attitudes with regards to the other, and learning together better ways of dealing with conflict.

TOOLS

Misriyati uses non-formal education as the means to explore the knowledge, skills and values related to peaceful living. We depend on experiential learning and learning by doing.

REFERENCES

Constitution of the United Nations Educational, Scientific, and Cultural Organisation

Galtung Johan, 2004, *Transcend and Transform: An Introduction to Conflict Work*, Paradigm Publishers, Boulder, USA

Haavelsrud Magnus, *The Substance of Peace Education*, Department of Education, Norwegian University of Technology and Science, N-7491, Trondheim

http://education.stateuniversity.com/pages/2314/Peace-Education.html

http://www.eycb.coe.int/compass/en/chapter_1/1_2.html#121

http://www.peace.ca/peaceeducationtheory.htm

http://www.ppu.org.uk/learn/peaceed/pe_ednetcurriculum.html

http://www.un.org/cyberschoolbus/peace/frame2.htm

Page James, 2008, *Peace Education: Exploring Ethical and Philosophical Foundations*

Reardon Betty A, *Peace Education: A Review and Projection*

www.ppu.org.uk/learn/peaceed/pe_childern_books.htmls

Building a Community of Learners

A Way of Educating the World

Arcie G Mallari

After receiving my college degree in November 2005, I chose to live in one of the biggest dumpsites in the Philippines called Payatas. My life became intimately intertwined with the lives of young men and women who lived in poverty. It was at Payatas that I met youths who dreamt of being jeepney[116] drivers' assistants, tricycle drivers, or housemaids. Getting a college education like I had achieved was a reality that they did not fathom.

Joms was one of these youths. He was a 15-year-old, third-year high school student who was having a terribly difficult time reading an English prayer book that I had handed him during our community prayer. Needless to say, he could not even comprehend what he was reading. I cannot imagine how he was dealing with his academic subjects such as Mathematics and Science in school, since they were mostly in the English language. I wondered if it was only Joms or he was just a part of Philippines' education problems. This inquiry inspired and moved me to seek the answer.

As I researched facts that would assist me in discovering our country's education status, appalling statistics became evident before me: while quantitatively, the Department of Education manages to maintain an average classroom-student ratio of 1:50; a textbook-student ratio of 1:1; and teacher-student ratio of 1:50,[117] qualitatively, we have only managed to increase the net enrolment ratio in primary education from 85 per cent in 1991 to 90 per cent in 2003. The percentage of students starting grade one who reach up to grade six has barely progressed from over 68 per cent in 1991 to under 70 per cent in 2003. And our literacy rates[118] of 15 to 24-year-olds, which measure quality and learning achievements, dropped from 97 per cent in 1990 to 94 per cent in 2003. Statistics show that the growth of education should not only be considered in terms of infrastructure but that it should go in tandem with programmes addressing the gap of literacy and quality education. The lack of quality education predicted a spate of adversities in our battle for national and economic development.

In a larger scale, while there are still 50 million children out of school in South and West Asia, primary enrolment is nearing 75 per cent.[119] In both regions, there is a strong correlation between low enrolment rates and the incidence of poverty. Enrolling children in school is a major concern – retaining them in school is a different issue. Countries like Mozambique, Rwanda, Malawi, Equatorial Guinea, and Chad in Sub-Saharan Africa have the highest drop out rates: more that 60 per cent of their students fail to reach their last grade.[120] Although the total number of illiterate adults (both men and women over the age of 15) dropped from an estimated 962 million in 1990 to 887 million in 2000, more than 20 per cent are still illiterate. In that year, 71 per cent of the world's illiterates were from Eastern and Southern Asia combined.[121] Educational quality and literacy concerns facing other regions are a huge stumbling block to sustainable economic and social development.

Education is the heart and soul of development. History can attest that those countries that have made a big leap out of poverty were those nations that have invested the most on education. Education[122] enables people to use and extend their capabilities, develop skills, improve their livelihoods, and increase their earning potential. And it also empowers them to participate in the decision-making process as well as in the transformation of their lives and societies. A quality education can help people to foster industrial and agricultural innovations and improve a community's capacity to make use of their environment in a sustainable way. By the same token, people can learn how to take care of themselves and that of their families. Thus, education contributes to the incremental realisation of other rights.

The importance of quality education for individual, community and national development is reflected in its recognition as a human right. The right to a primary education is enshrined in the *Universal Declaration of Human Rights* (1948: Article 26), which states that, at least in the primary and fundamental stages of a person's life, education should be free and directed to the full development of the human personality and the strengthening of human rights and fundamental freedoms. The Philippines is a signatory to the *UN Millennium Declaration* adopted during the Millennium Summit in September 2000. Within a 15-year timeline from 1990 to 2015, our country has committed to the pursuit of 8 major goals and 18 targets based on 48 indicators, within which the goal of achieving universal primary education (Goal 2-UPE) is included. Unfortunately, we are, however, significantly behind the targets. If we as a nation would want to eliminate poverty, then, we need to start investing on education.

After realising the importance of education and its impact on humanity, in April 2007, I created a non-governmental organisation called *Silid Aralan* (*Learning Room*),[123] whose aim is to empower children by facilitating discovery of their own fullest potential, developing their love for learning and discovering the purpose of their lives. We created partnerships among parents, schools, local government, and local business sectors in implementing the *Silid Aralan* educational programme for students considered academically challenged.[124] The programme started off with forty students from primary level.

Through Silid Aralan's partnership with the local government and parents in the community, it was possible to build the first Sil*id Aralan Community of Learners Centre*,[125] while engaging business sectors to donate paint and other construction materials needed. There were also school supplies donated. Volunteers from university and the community approached us to teach and tutor children in the centre. They used a learning methodology developed by *Silid Aralan* specifically for the children.

The learning methodology is known as *Silid Aralan Learning Technology* (SALT). It is premised on the Theory of Multiple Intelligences developed by Howard Gardner which postulates that learning is enhanced when teaching is deliberately built around not just two (2) intelligences (linguistic and logical-mathematical), but around other types of intelligence as well: musical, visual-spatial, bodily-kinesthetic, interpersonal, intra-personal and naturalist. Likewise, it has valid measures of an individual's learning style (Dunn and Dunn Learning Style) that calls for a matching teaching style for optional learning results. Hence, this learning methodology necessitates a kind of teaching whose strength lies in the careful analysis of students' learning styles and the training of teachers who can provide conditions/activities calculated to fit such characteristics

After one year, the so called 'academically challenged students' are now considered 'academic achievers' (i.e. students on the top-ten list of their classes) by their school. In addition, the village government created resolutions to support the education of the children providing free utilities in *Silid Aralan Community of Learners Centre,* as well as incentives to business owners who have donated to and shared resources in the programme. Parents, who were initially apprehensive, are now cooperating in maintaining the learning centre and encouraging their children to attend school after seeing the results of the programme.

Statistics and challenges mentioned earlier only tell us the extent of the work that needs to be done between now and 2015. It tells us the work that should be done by all of us: government, private sectors and civil society. And this is where *Silid Aralan* is taking its place – to bring together local governments, business sectors, schools and parents in educating and empowering children in the community. We are all working together in achieving quality education and peace for the whole of humanity.

future as well as to development on a global level. Education will utilise otherwise wasted potential and redirect it into a constructive path. On a global level, this will translate into better understanding and respect of other cultures. Many people are unaware of the different ways education could be perceived. Education needs to be improved on both a micro and a macro level.

Traditionally, there have been attempts to improve education systems around the world. However, developed countries have been able to successfully improve their education systems since they have the money, resources, and time to spend on the enterprise, whereas developing countries (ranging from Ghana to Lebanon) are still struggling to maintain stable nations. Therefore, people on the global level have a responsibility to assist their brothers and sisters from other parts of the world so everybody can receive a better education. In order to execute a practical and effective plan to improve education systems worldwide, people should begin inside at their own homes. Simple actions by families to become better aware of their surroundings, such as helping in local shelters, joining NGOs, and promoting awareness of current issues, are stepping stones to uniting the people for the cause of education. Giving assistance to a single individual is tantamount to helping humanity on a global level. Regardless of wealth, health, gender or race, everyone has the right to receive a top-quality education.

Notes

1. For a comprehensive history of the struggles over human rights, see Paul Lauren's *The Evolution of International Human Rights*, 1998.
2. O'Connell Davidson, Julia, 2005, *Children in the Global Sex Trade*, Polity Press: Cambridge, p.10
3. Child Wise, 2006, *Structural Causes of CSEC* 1
4. The Universal Declaration of Human Rights
5. *Ibid*
6. Ramesh Thakur, 'From National to Human Security', *Asia-Pacific Security: The Economics-Politics Nexus*, 1997
7. United Nations Development Programme
8. See Jorge Nef, *Human Security and Mutual Vulnerability: The Global Political Economy of Development and Underdevelopment*, 1999; also George MacLean, 'The Changing Perception of Human Security; Coordinating National and Multilateral Responses; The United Nations and the New Security Agenda', 1998
9. Kofi Annan, *Report of the Secretary-General on the Work of the Organisation,* General Assembly Official Records Fifty-fifth Session Supplement No.1 (A/55/1), United Nations, New York, 2000
10. NATO Strategic Concept
11. OSCE strategy to address the threats to the security and stability in the 21 Century, adopted at the OSCE Ministerial Council meeting in Maastricht, December 2003
12. Ogata, Sadako, *'Human Security a Refugee Perspective'*, Keynote speech at the Ministerial Meeting on Human Security Issues of the 'Lysoen Process', Group of Governments, Bergen, Norway, 19 May 1999
13. See in details: Gary King and Christopher J L Murray, 'Rethinking Human Security', in *Political Science Quarters*, Volume 116, N.4, 2001-2
14. *Ibid*

15. Ljubomir D Frckoski, *International Human Rights Law*, Magor, Skopje, 2005, p.315
16. The Maoists, also known as the Communist Party of Nepal, launched armed guerrilla warfare against the government and monarchy of Nepal. The former won a national election in April 2008 and now hold the majority in the Constituent Assembly – the current Prime Minister of Nepal is the leader of the Maoist party.
17. Security forces were made up of police and the Nepali Army, who were then loyal to King Gyanendra and were deployed across the country to fight a guerrilla war and quell Maoist uprisings.
18. http://www.un.org/children/conflict/english/conflicts.html
19. The *Optional Protocol to the Convention on the Rights of the Child* on the involvement of children in armed conflict was adopted by the UN General Assembly in 2000 and entered into force in 2002. It was ratified by Nepal on 3 January 2007.
20. Child Workers in Nepal (CWIN), a leading NGO in Nepal, estimates 40,000 children were displaced due to the conflict.
21. Dalits are regarded as untouchables in the Nepali caste system and often face caste-based discrimination.
22. Human Rights Watch (2007) *Children in the Ranks; the Maoists Use of Child Soldiers in Nepal*
23. Cantonments were set up after a peace agreement in November 2006 for Maoist combatants, who were also required to disarm.
24. *UNMIN, UNICEF, Save the Children,* and several local NGOs are undertaking *Disarmament, Demobilization and Reintegration (DDR)* of former combatants
25. http://www.unmultimedia.org/radio/english/detail/64299.html
26. After the people's movement in April 2006 and the ensuing/ subsequent ceasefire, peace talks led to national elections in April 2008.
27. The youth wing of the Maoist party, mostly active in Kathmandu, and made up largely of soldiers who were demobilised. Their activities have been widely criticised for being violent and illegal.
28. The National Plan of Action is currently in draft form and has been prepared by the Ministry of Peace and Reconstruction with support from UNICEF, NGOs and civil society to guide the reintegration of children.
29. Recommendations of the *Security Council Working Group on Children and Armed Conflict*
30. Tuk Tuk is a motor vehicle. It is a motorized version of the traditional rickshaw or velotaxi, a small three-wheeled cart driven by a person. Source: http://en.wikipedia.org/wiki/Tuk-tuk_taxi
31. 'Peace Built from Bottom Up "Begins with Every One of Us", Says

Secretary-General to "Mondial Des Enfants" Festival'. Source:http://www.un.org/News/Press/docs/2000/20000626.sgsm7463.doc.html

32. *Fresh and wet earth, dry and burning earth, I am to take to you lovingly, I am to take to you in suffering,* Jorge Debravo *(You, the Earth)*
33. See: http://www.un.org/events/humanrights/udhr60/declaration.shtml
34. This right was further formalised in the 1976 *International Covenant on Civil and Political Rights.*
35. Fahmy, Eldin, 2006, *Young Citizens: Young People's Involvement in Politics and Decision*, Ashgate Publishing Ltd, p.1
36. Pierre Claude, Richard and Weston, Burns H, (Ed), (2/E, 1992), 2006, *Human Rights in the World Community: Issues and Action*, University of Pennsylvania Press, Philadelphia, p.231
37. *Rio Declaration*, approved of during the Reunion of the United Nations on Environment and Development in June 1991, in the City of Rio de Janeiro, Brazil
38. See: http://www.unep.org/Documents.Multilingual/Default.asp?DocumentID=78&ArticleID=1163
39. On 25 June 1998, at the *Fourth 'Environment for Europe' Ministerial Conference* in Aarhus, Denmark, 35 countries and the European Union signed the new *United Nations Economic Commission for Europe (UNECE) Convention on Access to Information, Public Participation in Decision-Making, and Access to Justice in Environmental Matters* (generally known as *the Aarhus Convention*).
40. *The Aarhus Convention: An Implementation Guide,* 2000, United Nations Economic Commission for Europe (UNECE), United Nations Publication, New York and Geneva
41. Source: World Youth Report 2007, United Nations, Department of Economic and Social Affairs
42. *Idem*
43. See: http://www.un.org/esa/socdev/unyin/wyr07.htm
44. Agenda 21, Chapter 25: Children and Youth in Sustainable Development, 25.7
45. http://www.righttoenvironment.org
46. Zukin, Cliff, Keeter Scott, Andolina Molly, Jenkins Krista, 2006, *A New Engagement?: Political Participation, Civic Life, and the Changing*, Oxford University Press, New York, p.4
47. Griffin, James, 2008, On Human Rights, Oxford University Press, New York, p.97
48. 'The World Food Crisis' New York Times, Editorial, 10 April 2008, online available at: http://www.nytimes.com/2008/04/10/opinion/10thu1.html?_r=1&scp=4&sq =food%20crisis&st=cse
49. In July 2008, it was estimated that 1.2 million people were in need of

urgent food supplies in Kenya. Other neighbouring countries, such as Ethiopia and Somalia, were worse off. 'Food Crisis Looms in East Africa', BBC Online available at:
http://news.bbc.co.uk/2/hi/africa/7520286.stm
50. 'Towards Achieving Food Security in Kenya' Presentation by Joseph Kinyua, Permanent Secretary, Ministry of Agriculture, at the Conference *Assuring Food and Nutrition Security in Africa by 2020: Prioritizing Action, Strengthening Partners, and Facilitating Partnerships*, 1-4 April 2004 Kampala Uganda, online available at:
http://www.ifpri.org/2020africaconference/program/day1summaries/kinyua.pdf
51. *The Universal Declaration of Human Rights*, online available at:
http://www.unhchr.ch/udhr/lang/eng.htm
52. http://www.actionaid.org/main.aspx?PageID=24
53. http://www1.umn.edu/humanrts/instree/z1afchar.htm
54. Protocol to the African Charter on Human And Peoples' Rights on The Rights of Women in Africa, online available at:
http://www.achpr.org/english/_info/women_en.html
55. 'Across the Globe, Empty Bellies Bring Rising Hunger', New York Times, 18 April 2008, online available at:
http://www.nytimes.com/2008/04/18/world/americas/18food.html?pagewanted=1&sq=food%20crisis&st=cse&scp=10
56. 'Food for thought' Economist, 27 March 2008, online available at:
http://www.economist.com/world/international/displaystory.cfm?story_id=10925518
57. Refer to footnote 8.
58. For a profile of Diana Onyonyi, refer to an article in a Kenyan daily 'Girl 14 Steps into Ongeri's (Minister for Education) Shoes', *Daily Nation* 7 January 2009, online available at:
http://www.nation.co.ke/News/-/1056/510534/-/item/0/-/gv0it5/-/index.html
59. See 'Kenyan youths demand to be included in food talks', *ActionAid News Release*, online available at:
http://www.actionaid.org/kenya/index.aspx?PageID=3416
60. See 'The Horn of Africa: tragedy of the decade?' *The Economist*, 30 October 2008, online available at:
http://www.economist.com/world/mideast-africa/displaystory.cfm?story_id=12517047
61. See for instance, 'Could GM Food Help Feed Africa?', BBC News, online available at: http://news.bbc.co.uk/2/hi/africa/7428789.stm
62. Justiciability, as defined by Jean Ziegler, the UN Special Rapporteur, is the possibility that a human right can be invoked before judicial and semi-judicial organisms that can determine whether the right has

or has not been violated, and can decide about the redemptive measures to be taken (*FLAN* 2008:7).

63. Monoculture cropping is the agricultural practice of cultivating only one single type of crop over a wide area with little consideration for domestic needs. Moreover, practices without diversity or dissension have adverse, long-term environmental consequences. In the last decades, monoculture cropping has produced a worldwide surplus of food that has depressed crop prices.
64. Cash crops attract demand in more developed countries, and hence have some export value. In other words, a cash crop is a crop grown for money – as opposed to subsistence crops, which are those fed to the producer's own livestock.
65. The Kaiser Family Foundation, July, 2008,*The Global HIV/AIDS Epidemic*. Washington DC, USA
66. UNAIDS, 2008, *2008 Report on the Global AIDS Epidemic*, WHO Library, Geneva, Switzerland
67. UNAIDS, 2008, *Key Facts by Region, 2008 Report on the Global AIDS Epidemic*, WHO Library Geneva, Switzerland
68. Population Reference Bureau, 2007, *2007 World Population Data Sheet*, USAID, Washington DC, USA
69. Alexander M, 'Information and Education Laws', in Dr Jayasuriya (Ed), 1995, HIV, Law, Ethics and Human Rights, UNDP, New Delhi, UNAIDS, 1997, p.54. Impact of HIV and sexual health education on the sexual behaviour of young people: A Review Update.
70. UNAIDS, *2008 Report on the Global AIDS Epidemic*, WHO Library, Geneva, Switzerland
71. Governments in the Group of Eight are: Canada, France, Germany, Italy, Japan, Russia, the United Kingdom, and the United States
72. www.ifmsa.org
73. www.medstudentsfightaids.org
74. Report of the UNAIDS Technical Consultation on Social Change Communication
75. National Research Council *et al*, 2005, *Growing up Global: The Changing Transitions to Adulthood in Developing Countries*, National Academies Press, Washington DC
76. Lown B, Bukachi F, Xavier R, 1998, *Health Information in the Developing World*, *Lancet* 352 (suppl. II):34–8S
77. http://www.internetworldstats.com/stats.htm
78. Ybarra M L, Bull S S, 2007, *Current Trends in Internet and Cell phone-based HIV Prevention and Intervention Programmes*, Curr HIV/AIDS Rep 4: 201-7
79. Borzekowski D L, Fobil J N, Asante KO, 2006, *Online Access by Adolescents in Accra: Ghanaian Teens' Use of the Internet for Health*

Information, Dev Psychol 2006, 42:450-458

80. Ybarra M L, Kiwanuka J, Emenyonu N, Bangsberg D R, 2006, *Internet use among Ugandan Adolescents: Implications for HIV Intervention*, PLoS Med 2006, 3: e433
81. European Society for Medical Oncology, 2002, *WHO and Six Publishers Launch Access to Research, Internet Initiative for Developing Countries*, Annals of Oncology 2002 13:641-645
82. Ybarra M L, Bull S S, 2007, *Current Trends in Internet and Cell phone-based HIV Prevention and Intervention Programmes*, Curr HIV/AIDS Rep 4: 201-7
83. Ybarra M L, Kiwanuka J, Emenyonu N, Bangsberg D R, 2006, *Internet Use among Ugandan Adolescents: Implications for HIV Intervention*, 2006, PLoS Med 3:e433
84. http://www.isoc.org/inet2001/CD_proceedings/G53/mobilepaper2.htm
85. This means that rights are not a privilege that some people have, but something all people are entitled to regardless of where they live, what caste they belong to, whether they are female or male (biologically), etc.
86. Rights have connections and reinforce each another. You cannot have the full potential of one right without another. For example, in order to achieve a right to health, you must also have the right to economic stability and to earn a wage.
87. This means that a hierarchy of rights cannot be created where some rights are considered more important than another. For instance, you cannot claim that the right to vote is more important the right to health.
88. These rights and freedoms cannot be challenged or taken away from a person and each person is born with the same rights.
89. Sexual Orientation is understood to refer to each person's capacity for profound emotional, affectional and sexual attraction to, and intimate and sexual relations with, individuals of a different gender or the same gender or more than one gender.
90. Gender Identity is understood to refer to each person's deeply felt internal and individual experience of gender, which may or may not correspond with the sex assigned at birth, including the personal sense of the body (which may involve, if freely chosen, modification of bodily appearance or function by medical, surgical or other means) and other expressions of gender, including dress, speech and mannerism.
91. Lefebvre, Henri, 1999, *A Revolução Urbana*, Belo Horizonte: Editora UFMG, p.81
92. UN GAOR, 43rd Sess., Supplement n. 8, addendum (A/43/8/Add.1)
93. UN-HABITAT, 2003, *The Challenge of Slums:* Global Report on Human

Settlements, UN Human Settlements Programme, Earthscan Publications, London and Sterling

94. UN-HABITAT, 2003, *The Challenge of Slums:* Global Report on Human Settlements, UN Human Settlements Programme, Earthscan Publications, London and Sterling
95. UN-HABITAT, 2003, *The Challenge of Slums:* Global Report on Human Settlements, UN Human Settlements Programme, Earthscan Publications, London and Sterling
96. Instituto Brasileiro de Geografia e Estatística (IBGE), 2001, *Census of 2000*, <http://www.ibge.gov.br>
97. Original text: *Gente humilde, discriminada, ignorada. [. . .] E aqui estou eu/sentado no chão do meu barraco/com minha dignidade em pedaços. /Minha mente está confusa/Eu não sei quem eu sou/Eu não sei o que fazer/Eu não sei se sou um homem ou um rato.*
98. Socio-economic diagnosis is prepared by the organisation *Habitus* in August 2005
99. It is usually considered that, although all human beings have the right to have a place to live and not to be evicted from that place, there are some prerogatives of ownership that can be denied to them, such as the possibility of selling their houses.
100. *Constituição Federal de 1988*, Art. 183 (Brazil); Lei No. 10.257, de 10 de julho de 2001, D.O.U. de 11.07.2001, Art. 9 (Brazil).
101. Original text: *Quando o oficial de justiça chegou / lá na favela / e contra seu desejo / entregou prá seu Narciso / um aviso, uma ordem de despejo / assinada: / seu doutor, / assim dizia a petição: / dentro de dez dias / quero a favela vazia / e os barracos todos no chão / é uma ordem superior / [. . .] vou sair daqui / pra não ouvir o ronco do trator / pra mim não tem probrema / em qualquer canto me arrumo / de qualquer jeito me ageito / depois, o que eu tenho é tão pouco / minha mudança é tão pequena / que cabe no bolso de trás / mas essa gente aí, hein? / como é que faz?*
102. Santos, Boaventura de Sousa, 2002, "Can Law Be Emancipatory?" *Red Latino Americana de Antropología-Jurídica*. 10 July 2008 <http://www.geocities.com/relaju/souzasantos.htm>
103. Lei No. 10.257, de 10 de julho de 2001, D.O.U. de 11.07.2001, Art. 10 (Brazil)
104. Constituição Federal de 1988, Art. 5 , XXIII
105. Duarte, Madalena, 2004, "Novas e Velhas Formas de Protesto: o Potencial Emancipatório da Lei nas Lutas dos Movimentos Sociais", *Oficina do CES*, 210, Coimbra: Centro de Estudos Sociais, p.16
106. Expropriation is the governmental taking of an individual's property rights. According to Brazilian Law, in most cases the State must compensate the owners.
107. *Constituição Federal de 1988*, Art. 5 , XXIV

108. Freire Paulo, 2005, *Pedagogia do Oprimido*, Paz e Terra, Rio de Janeiro, p.59
109. *United Nations Universal Declaration of Human Rights* http://www.un.org/Overview/rights.html
110. Restorative Justice Online: http://www.restorativejustice.org/intro
111 Suffolk University, College of Arts & Sciences, Centre for Restorative Justice
http://www/suffolk.edu/cas/crj/r_justice.html
112. It is important to note that the *UDHR* have been refined repeatedly since their creation in 1948.
113. As an activist, I have participated in an amalgam of events – from state-wide protests against the Iraq war to participating in collegiate EID fast to raise awareness about the genocide in Darfur. While these events differ in size, organisation, and publicity, I have come to realise that effecting change is not just about joining nation-wide organisations and standing out (or even speaking out) in national arenas. Effecting change can be equally effective on a seemingly smaller scale.
114. In the Argentine system of education, 6- to 12-year-olds attend elementary school, while 13 to 17-year-olds must complete a 5-year high school education period. This is different from the usual US partition into elementary, middle, and high school cycles.
115. In the Argentine system of secondary-level education, students who fail to pass certain classes with an average of 6 or 7 out of 10 minimum (depending on the district) – which is equivalent to a B in the American system – need to take a series of demanding final examinations to be promoted to the next year of education. If a student fails more than 2 of their final examinations in a year, they need to retake all the courses that year.
116. One of the public utility vehicles in the Philippines
117. Department of Education, *Net Enrollment Ratio in Primary Education (2007)*, Philippines
118. Department of Education, *Functional Literacy, Education and Mass Media Survey* (FLEMMS) *2007*, Philippines
119. UNICEF, (1998), *Education State of the World's Children*, New York
120. UNESCO Education for All Global Monitoring Report 2007
121. Cited in International Literacy Institute (2000), *Education for All Thematic Study on Literacy and Adult Education*, UNESCO, Paris
122. Department of International Development (January 2001)
123. www.silidaralan.multiply.com
124. Academically challenged students – students who were repeatedly failing in their academic subjects (Mathematics, Science and English)
125. It is an After School centre where the students will be facilitated after their class in school.

Index

Acquisitive prescription, 126, 128
Agriculture, Kenya, 86, 91
Amnesty International, 19
Annan, Kofi, 37, 66, 74, 101, 169
Arhus Convention, 74, 79, 171
Armed conflict and youth, 8, 12, 41-43, 53-55, 57-58, 60, 156, 170-71
Article 1, 25-26, 63, 133
Article 2, 18
Article 3, 25-26, 55-57, 59, 63
Article 4, 26
Article 6, 18, 115-16
Article 11, 124
Article 12, 82, 148
Article 15, 88
Article 16, 13, 115-16, 119
Article 21, 72
Article 25, 88, 95, 124, 148
Article 26, 63, 105, 155, 164
Article 30, 25
Article 31, 116

Canadian Immigration and Refugee Protection Act, 24
Child-Safe Network, 63, 65, 67
Commercial Sexual exploitation of children (CSEC), 12, 26, 28
Council of Europe convention on Action against Trafficking in Human Beings 18-19, 33
CRC Optional Protocol, 55, 58, 170

Disarmament and demobilization in Nepal, 57
Domestic violence movement, 29

ECPAT, 28, 31

Fahmy, Eldin, 78, 171
FAO, 89, 93-94, 96, 97, 100, 102
Friends-International, 63-64, 66-67

Hague Agenda for Peace, 48, 51
HIV/AIDS, 13, 47, 64, 67, 85, 87, 104-12, 117, 138, 173-74
Home-based production project, 63-64
Homosexuality and human rights, 13, 116-19
Human rights education, 130, 151, 155, 164
Human security in foreign policies: Canada, Norway, Japan, 33
Human security, concept, 32-36

IDPs (Internal Displaced Persons), 43
International Labour Organisation, 21, 23
International Law, 20
Internet: tool for medical information, 13, 110

Justiciability, 96, 102, 173

Lauren, Paul, 8, 135, 169
Lederach, 42, 50
Lord's Resistance Army, 41
Lost childhood, 54

Maoists, Nepal, 56
Millennium Development Goals, 12, 47, 51, 91, 94-95, 125, 137-38, 140
Misryati, 160
Mokwena, 42, 45-47, 50

Nef, Josef

O'Connell Davidson, Julia, 31, 175
Ogata, Sadako, 37, 175

Peace Education, 13, 48, 49, 51, 154-61
Poles of Citizenship Program, 126, 127, 129-30
Positive peace, 155
Protection by law, 4, 7, 12, 22, 24-25, 36, 76, 104-05, 110, 117, 132, 134, 145
Protection of Minority Rights, 36
Protection Project, 22

Restorative justice, 13, 133-34, 176
Right to Food security, 94
Right to Food, 13, 88, 94-98, 100, 102
Rio Declaration on Environment and Development, 73, 79
Robinson, Mary, 6, 8, 97

Silid Aralan, 150, 164, 165
Street children in Cambodia:
development and Integration, prevention, protection, 63
Street children, 12, 62-64, 66-67

Thakur, Ramesh, 33, 43, 169
Trafficking and exploitation of human beings, 18
Trafficking and Recruitment/transport and forced labour, 19
Trafficking in Persons Report, 22
Trafficking in Women and Children, 18-19, 21, 23
Trafficking Laws: Canada, US, Armenia (absence of laws), 24-25, 34
Trafficking through deception, 19
Trafficking, definitions 18-19

UDHR: adoption, 17, 60, 71, 105, 115-16, 119, 148
UN Protocol to Prevent, suppress and punish trafficking in persons, 19
UNDP Human Development Report, 33, 37
UNFPA, 55
UNICEF, 45, 47, 51, 55, 58, 61, 97, 106, 177
United Nations Convention on the Rights of Children, 58

Virginia Floresca-Cawagas and Toh Swee-Him, 49

WHO, 94, 97, 103-04, 106, 108, 173-74
"Will You Listen", 54-55, 58

Youth participation in development, 12-13, 41-42, 46, 47, 49-51, 72, 75-76

Zovu, 41, 51